Dancing in the Light
Presents

I0473354

WONDERFUL WILD WYOMING

ENTANGLED TO DETANGLE: COLOR, PRAY & MEDITATE

ILLUSTRATIONS BY:

C. JUDIE WILLIAMS

Contact Information
C. Judie Williams
P.O. Box 1983
Riverton, WY 82501
Copyright © 2015 Carrie Judie Williams

Dancing In The Light

All rights reserved.

ISBN-13:978-0692549780

ISBN-10:0692549781

"Let them praise his name in the dance,"
Psalms 149:3
"And call upon me in the day of trouble:
I will deliver thee,
and thou shalt glorify me."
Psalms 50:15
This I pray will glorify thee,
O Lord, my heavenly father,
Thank you for allowing me to continue to
Dance in the Light of
Your Love and Grace.

DEDICATION
To my parents, Willie Paul & Martha Lou Brister,
Whose Adventurous Spirit brought them to settle for a large part of their
lives in Wonderful Wild Wyoming.
Their Adventurous Spirit Lives on in their children, grandchildren and
great-grandchildren.

ACKNOWLEDGEMENTS
My Husband Boyd Williams, Thank You for Loving Me.
Tom Kroenke, Thank You for Your Guidance and Encouragement.
Teesha Burt, Thank You for Your Generous Heart.

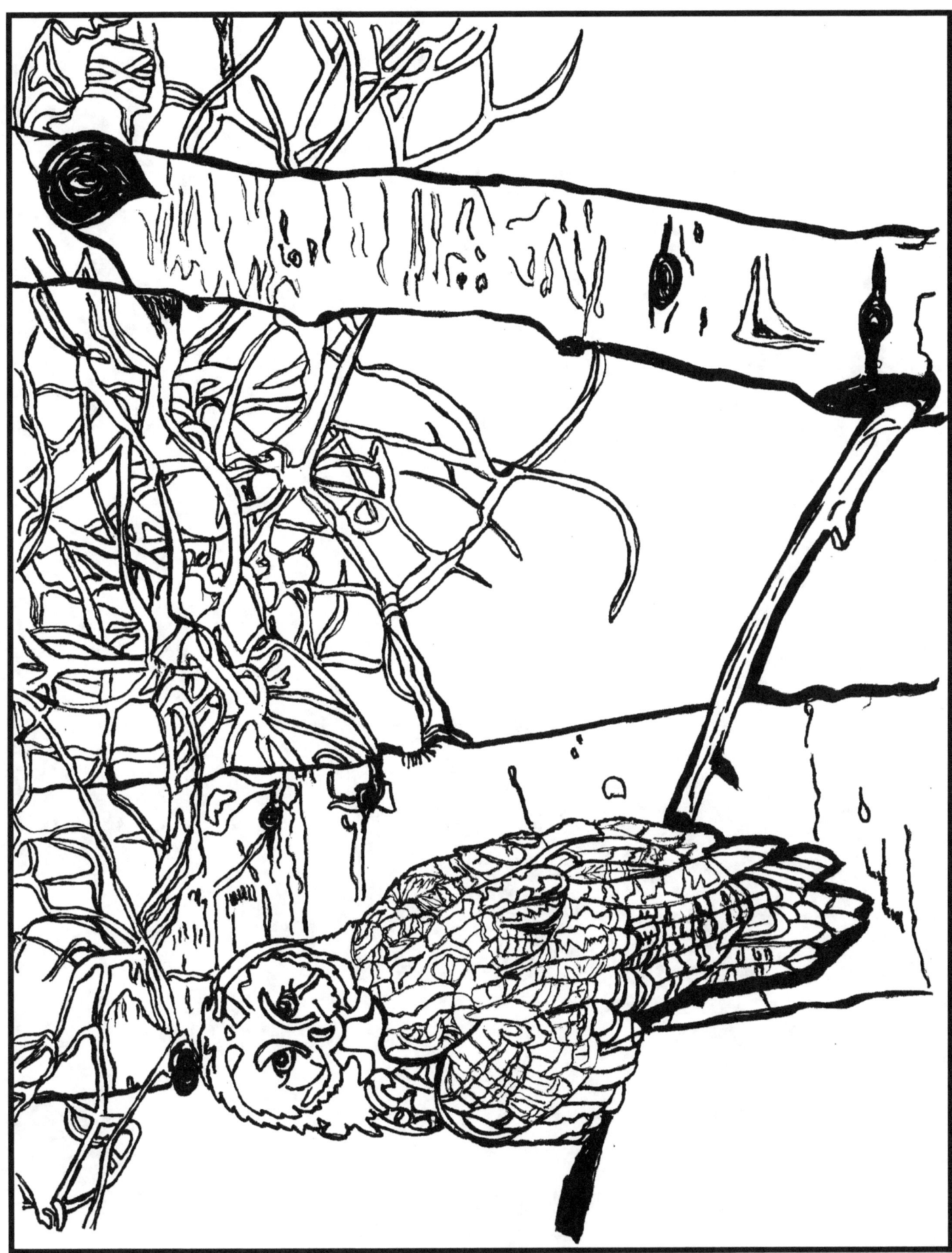

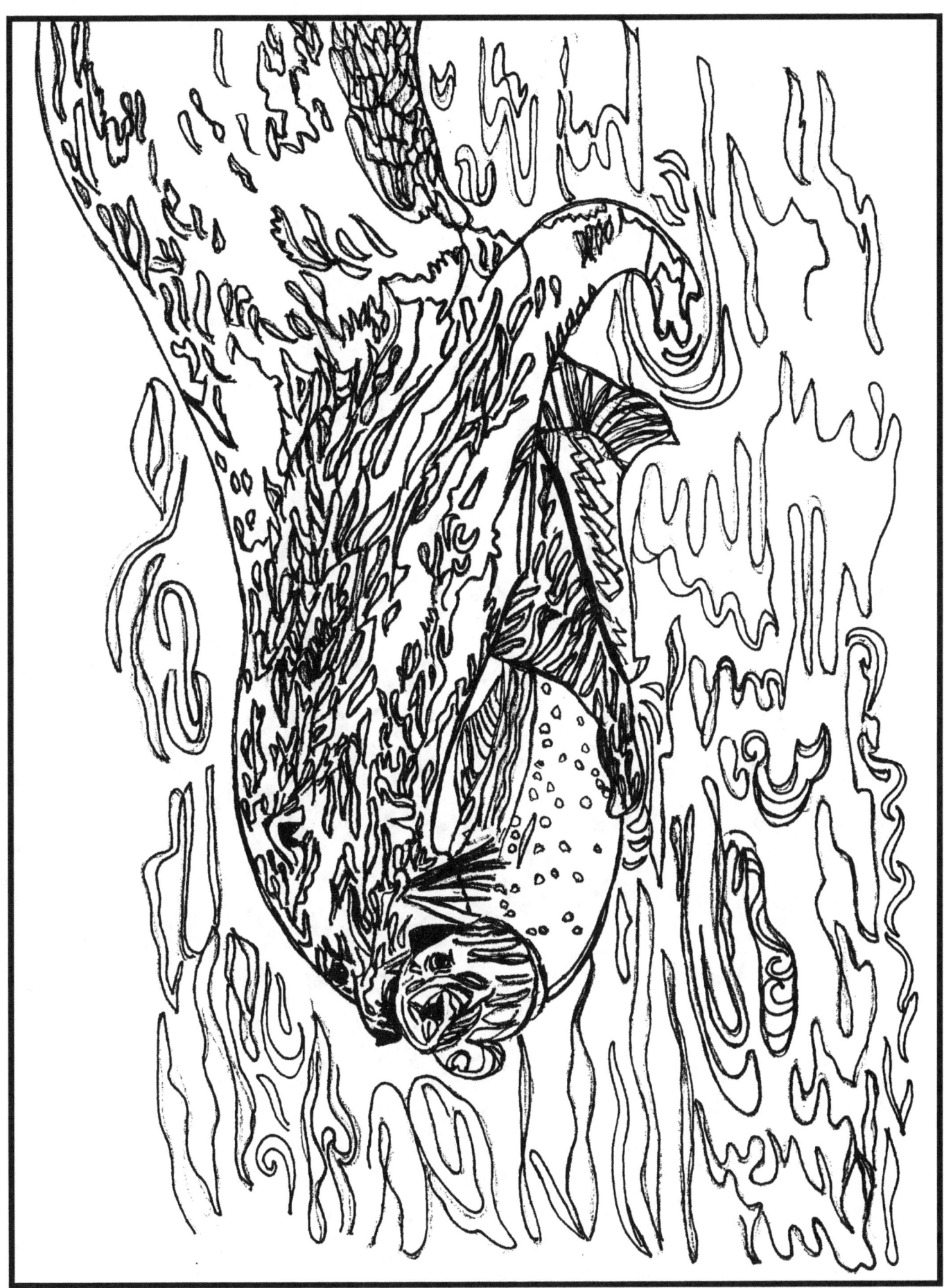

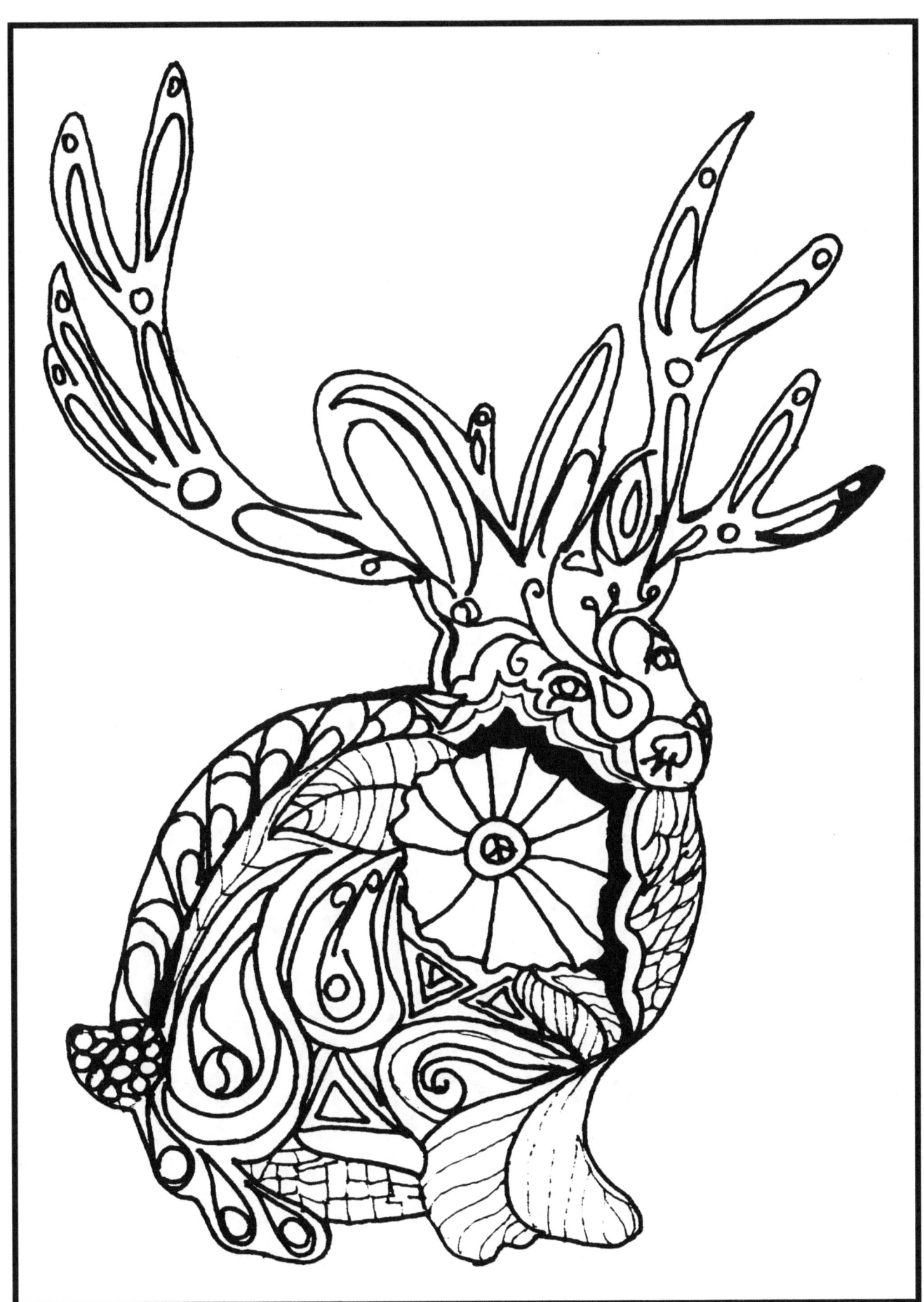

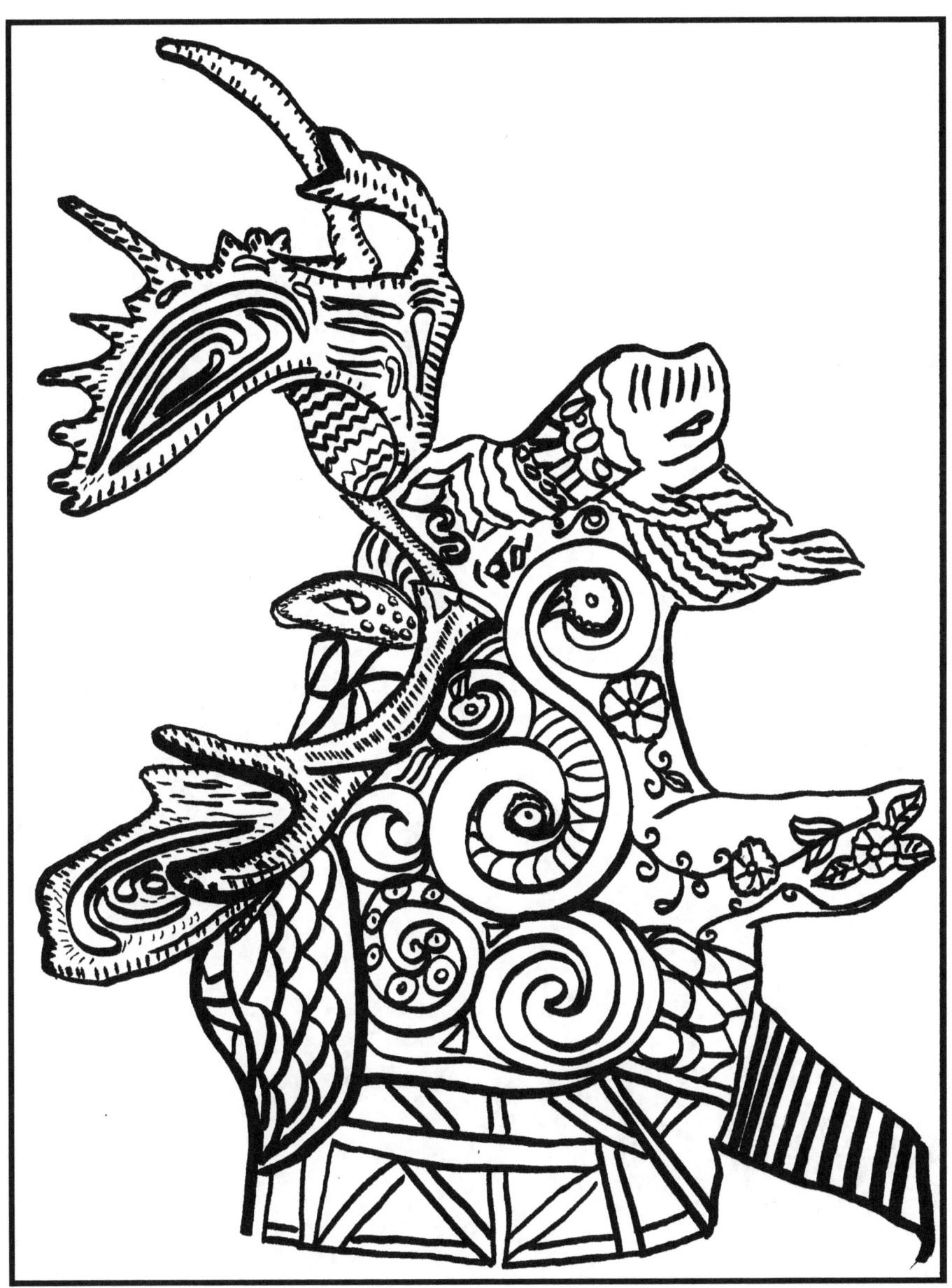

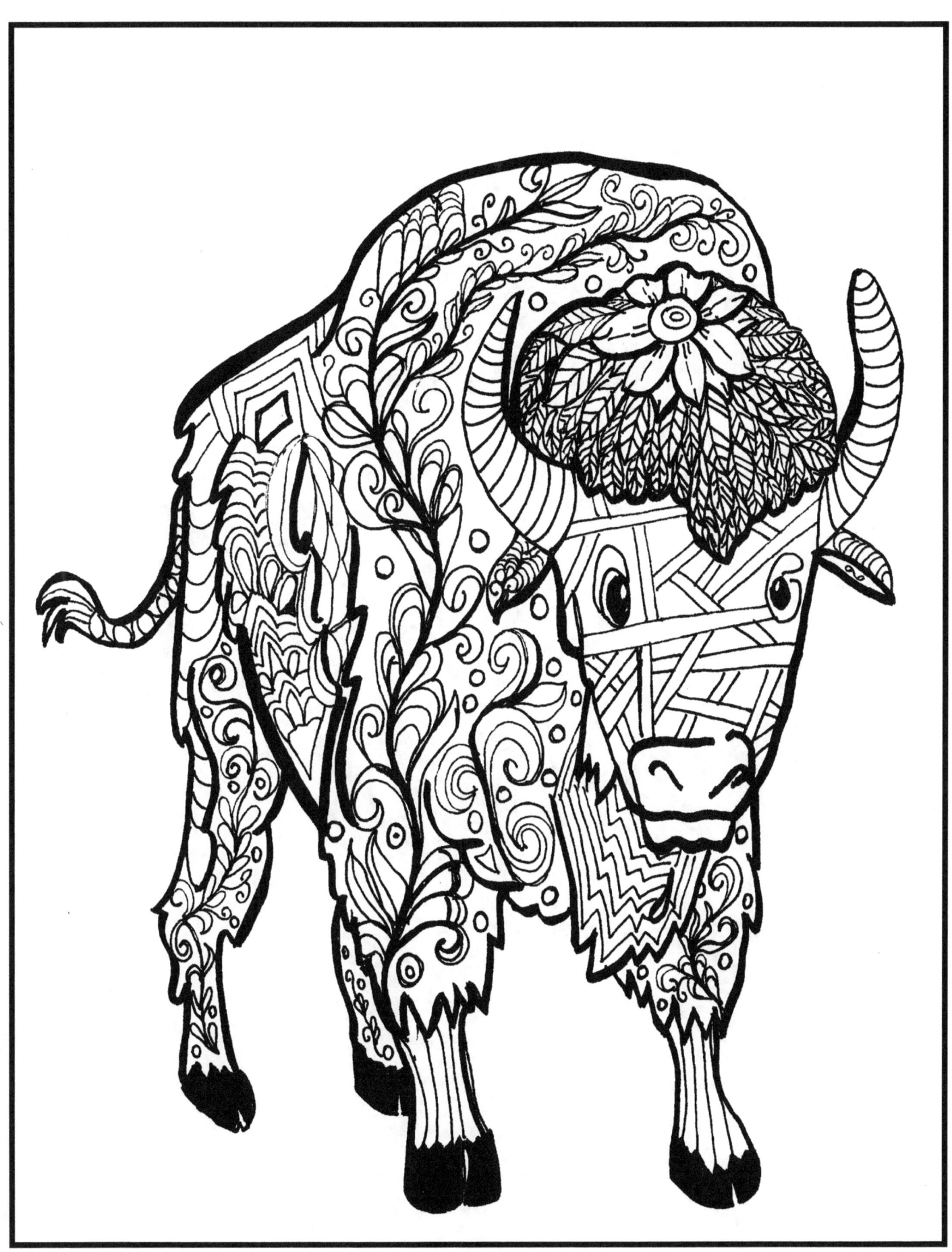

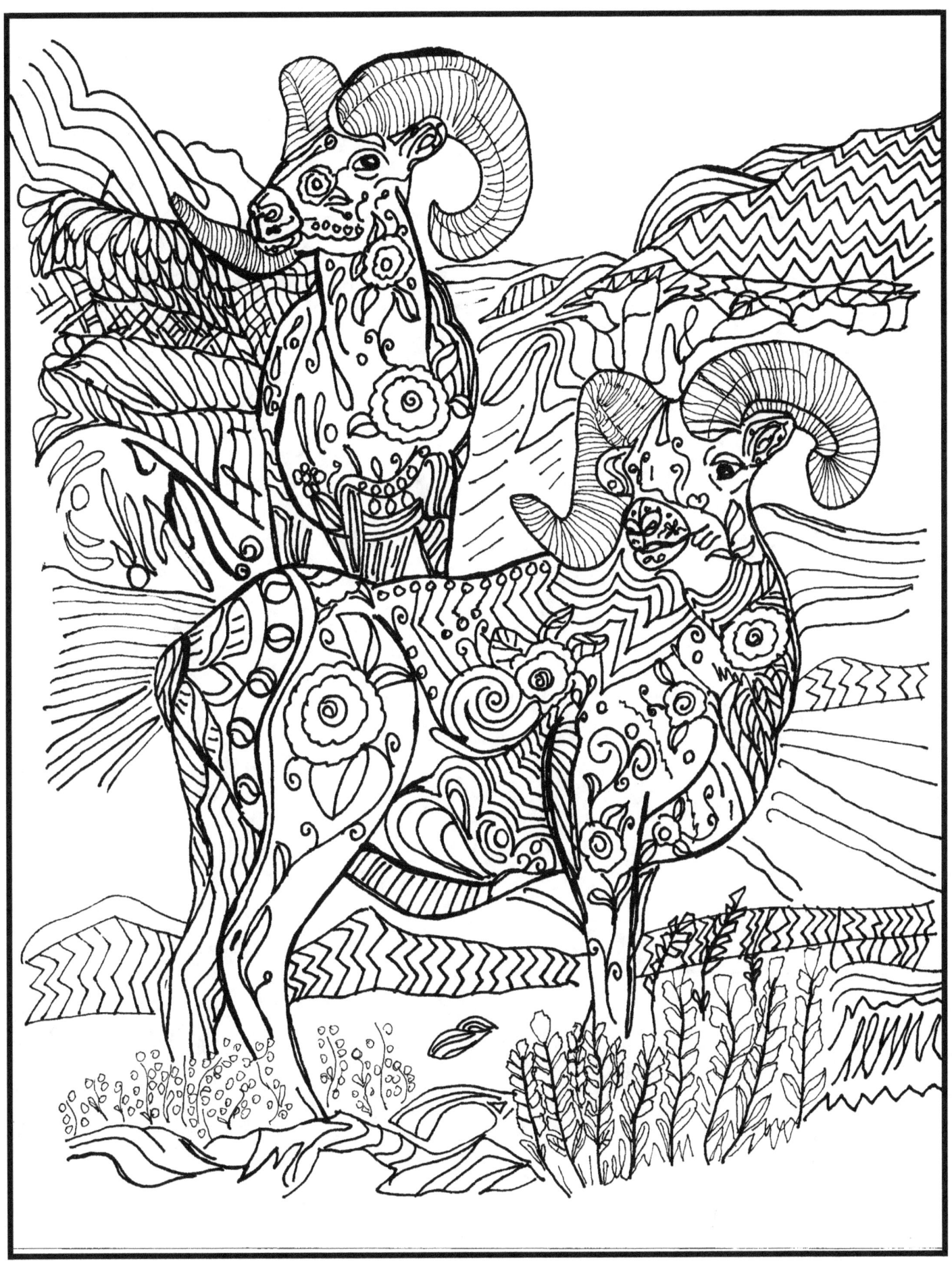

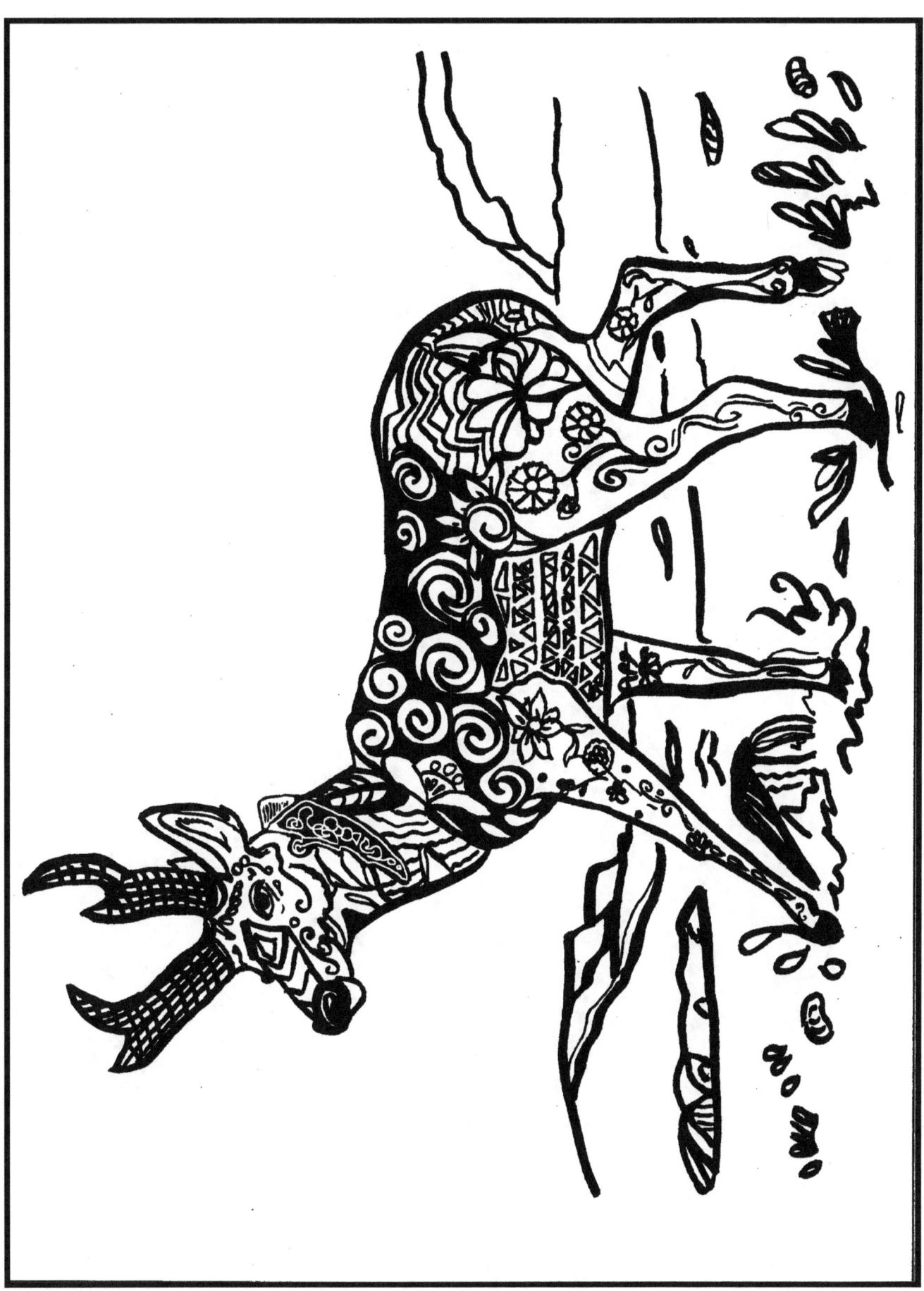

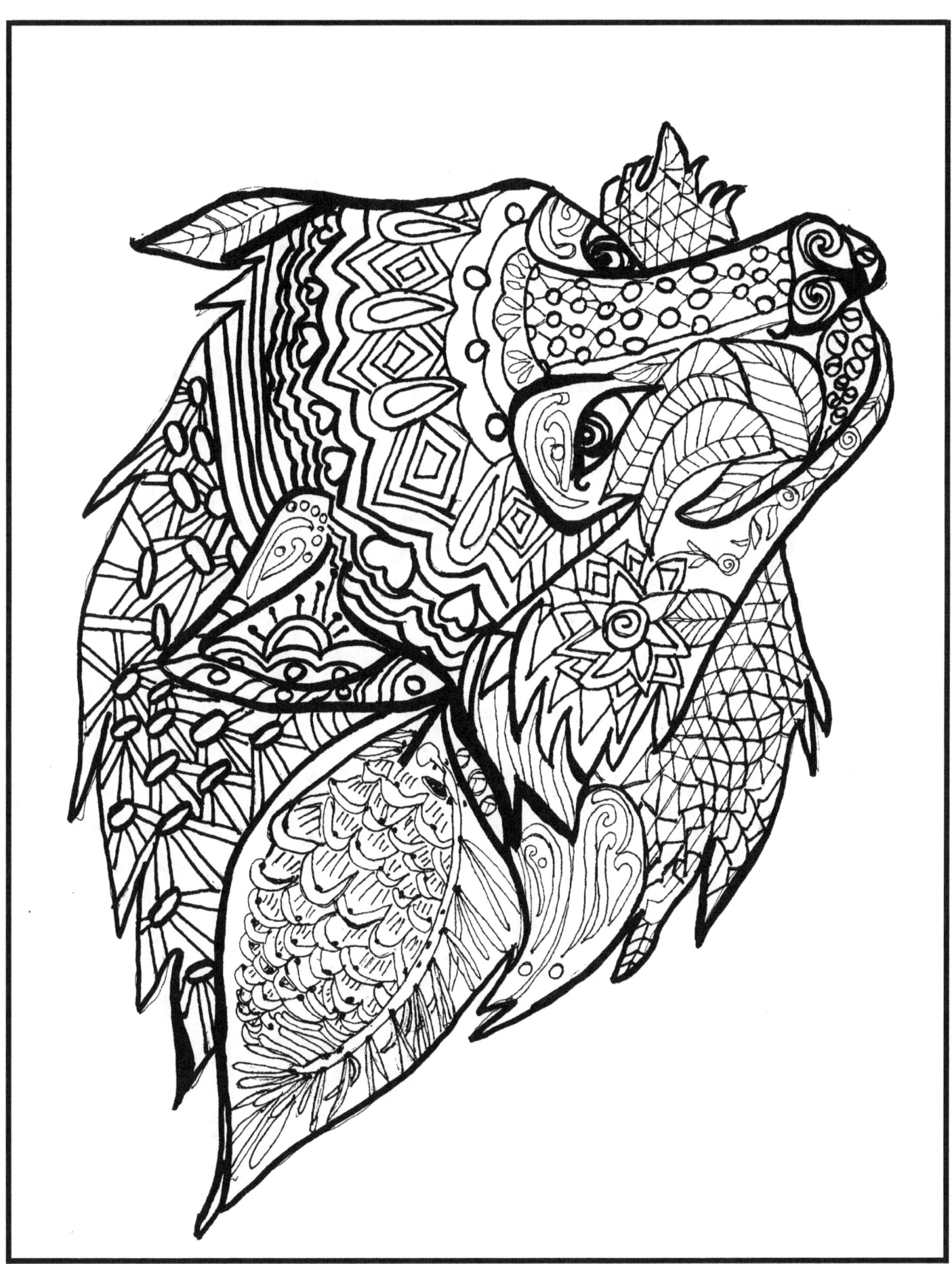

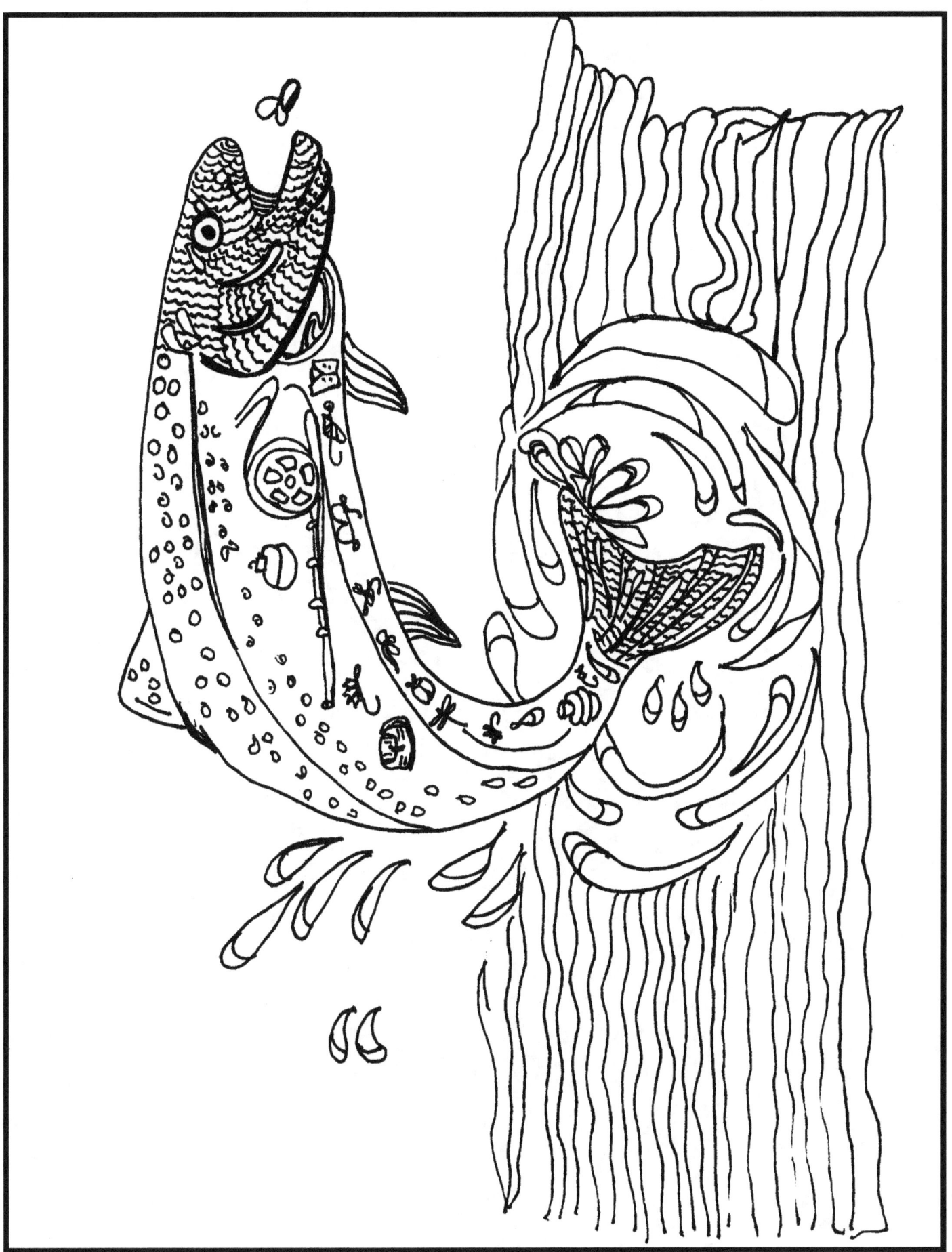

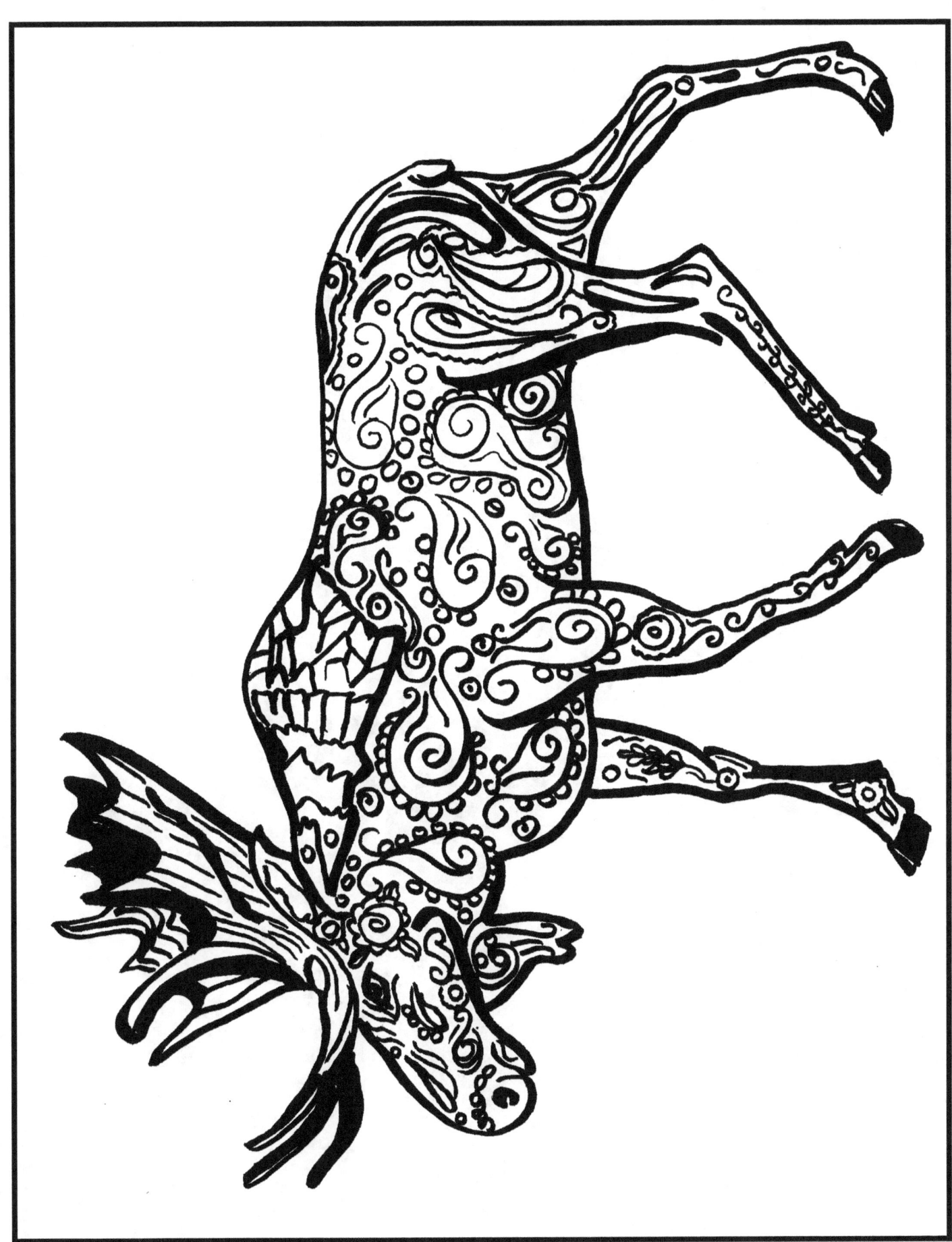

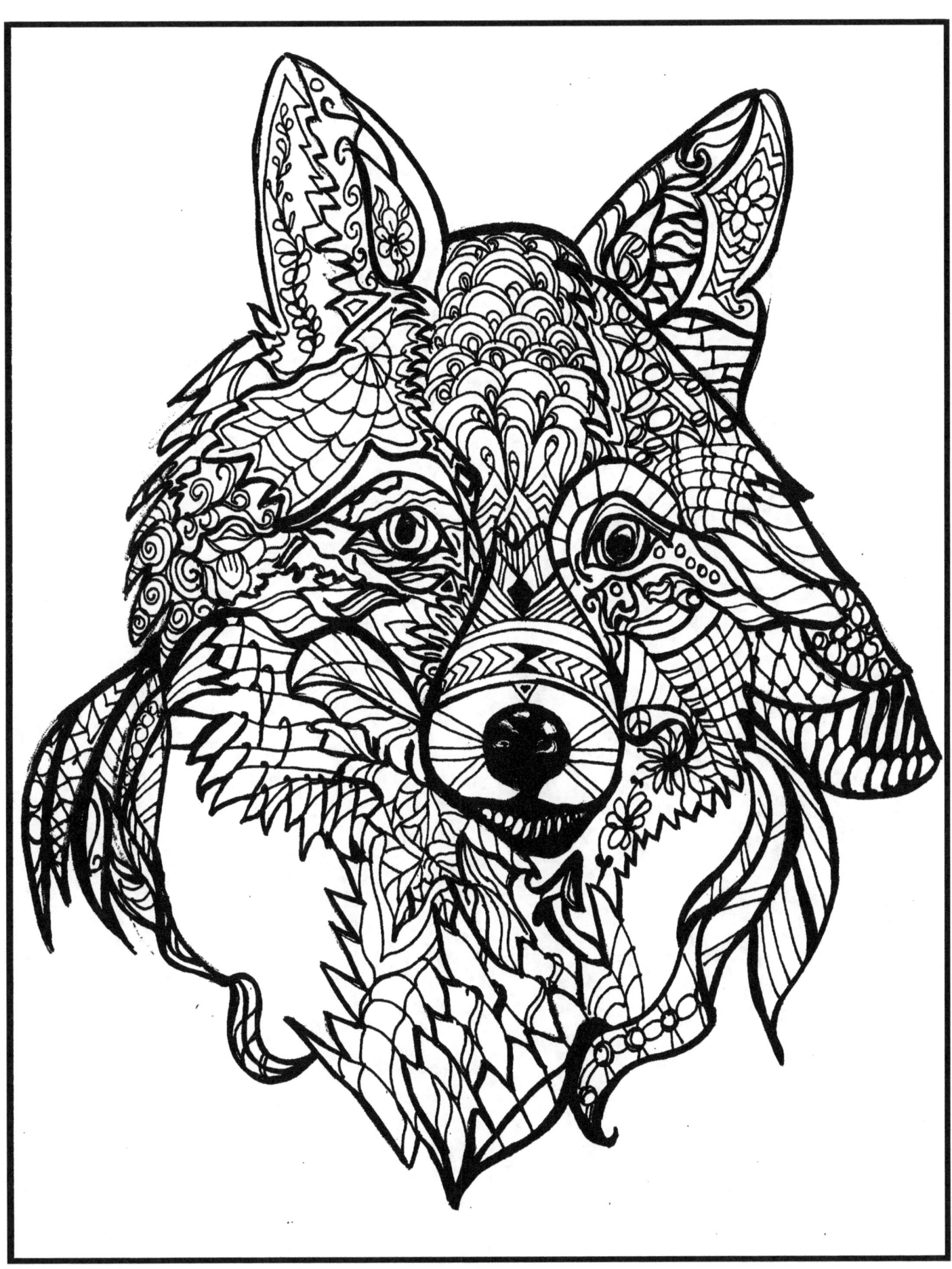

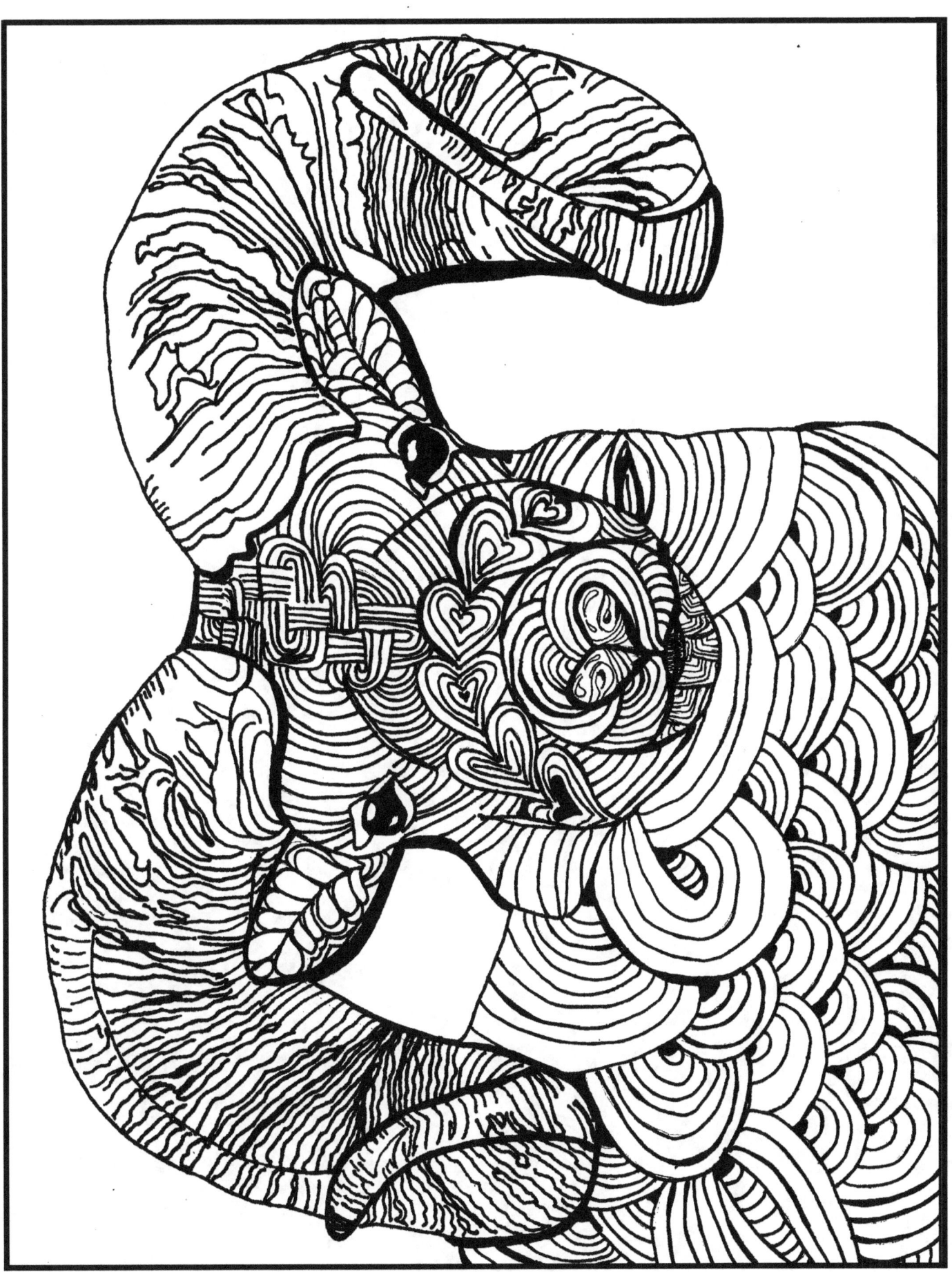

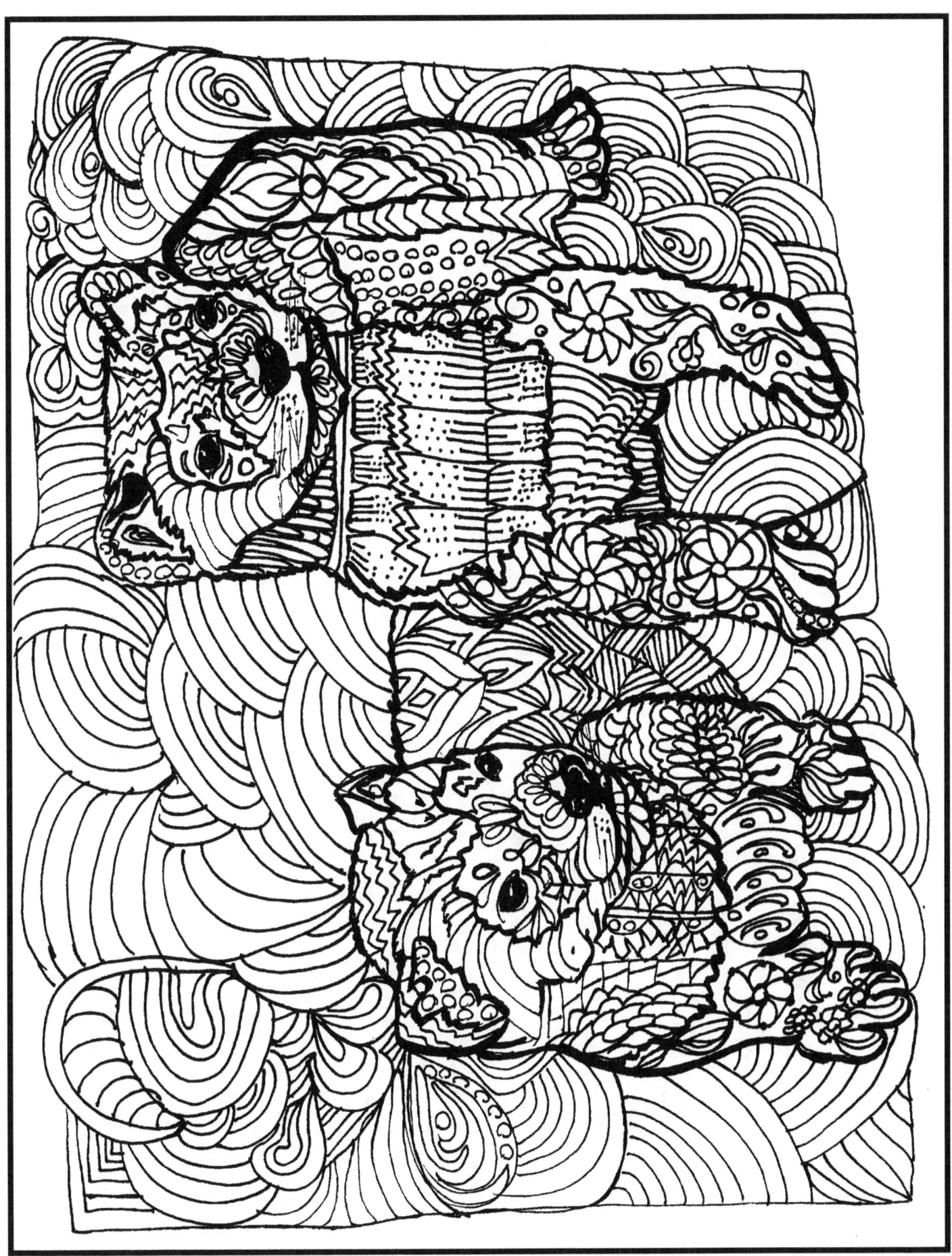

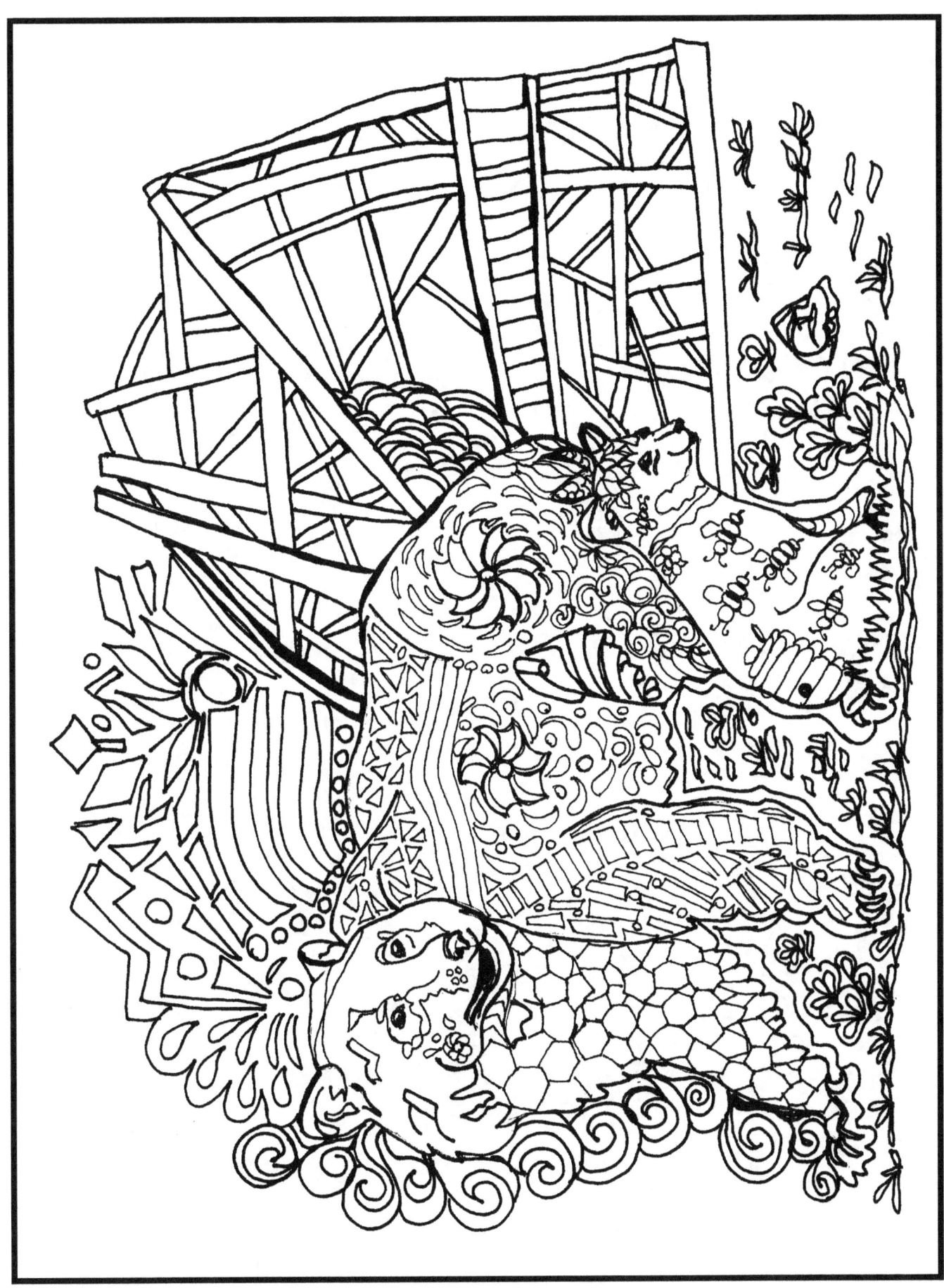

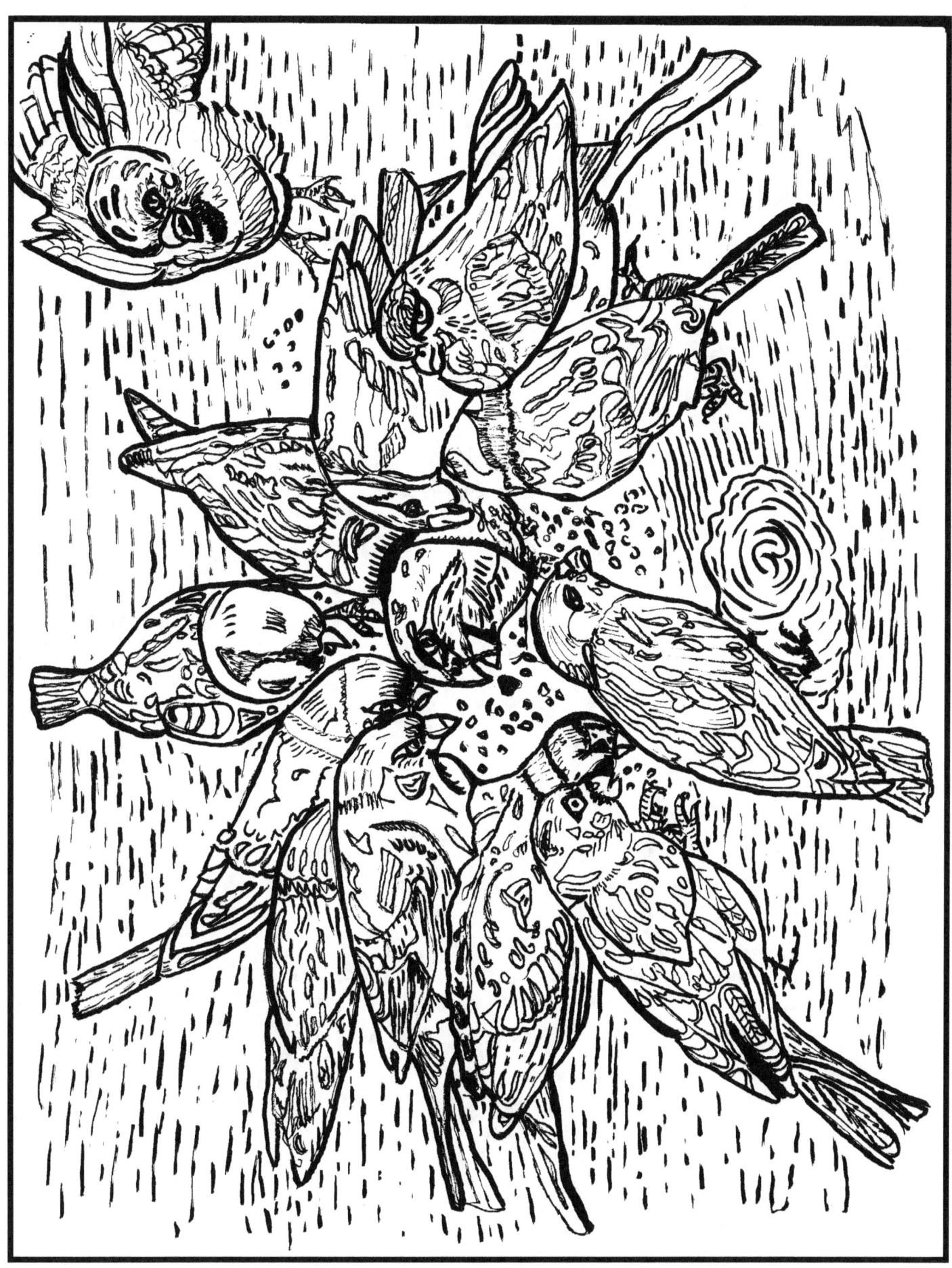

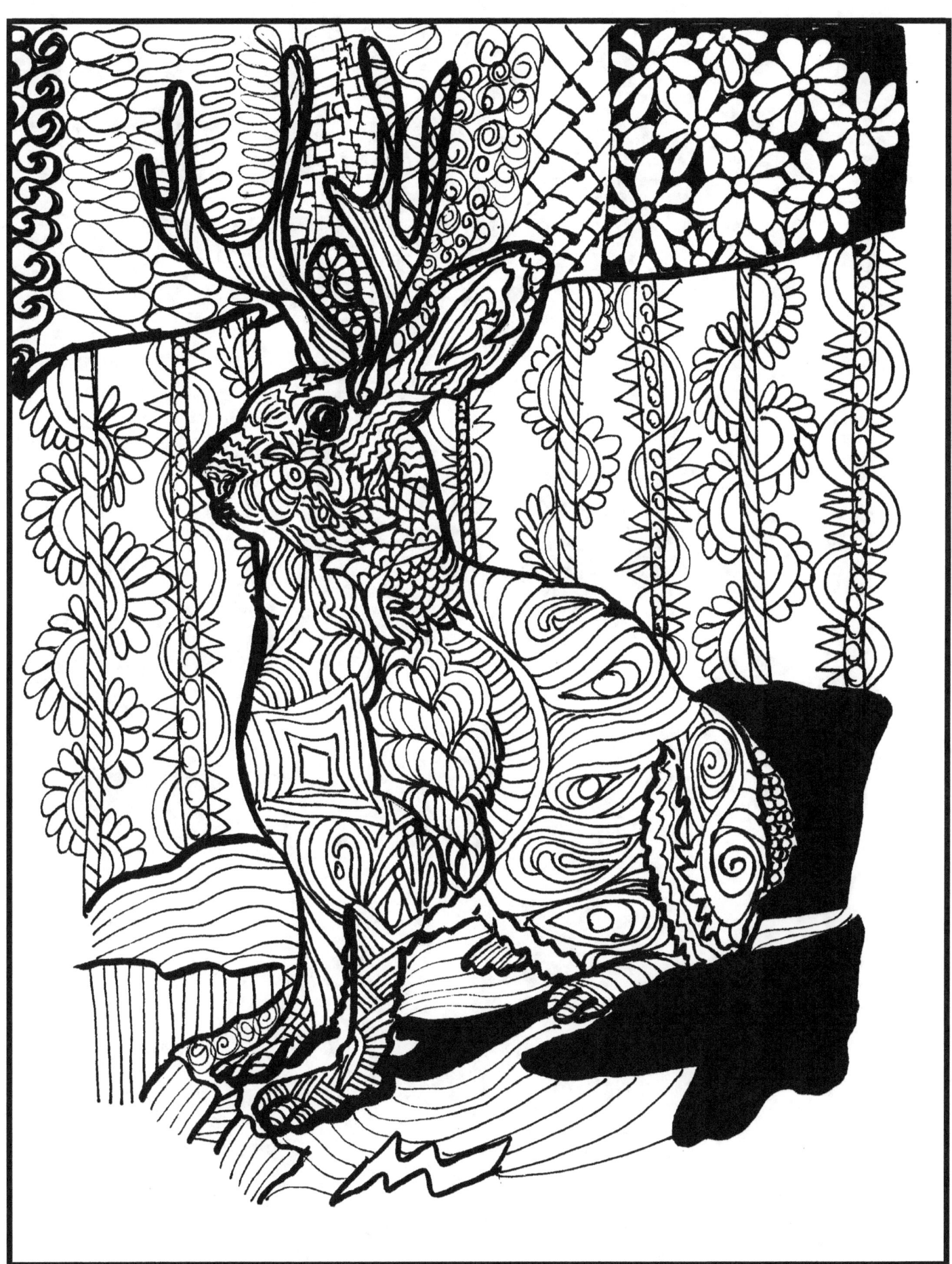

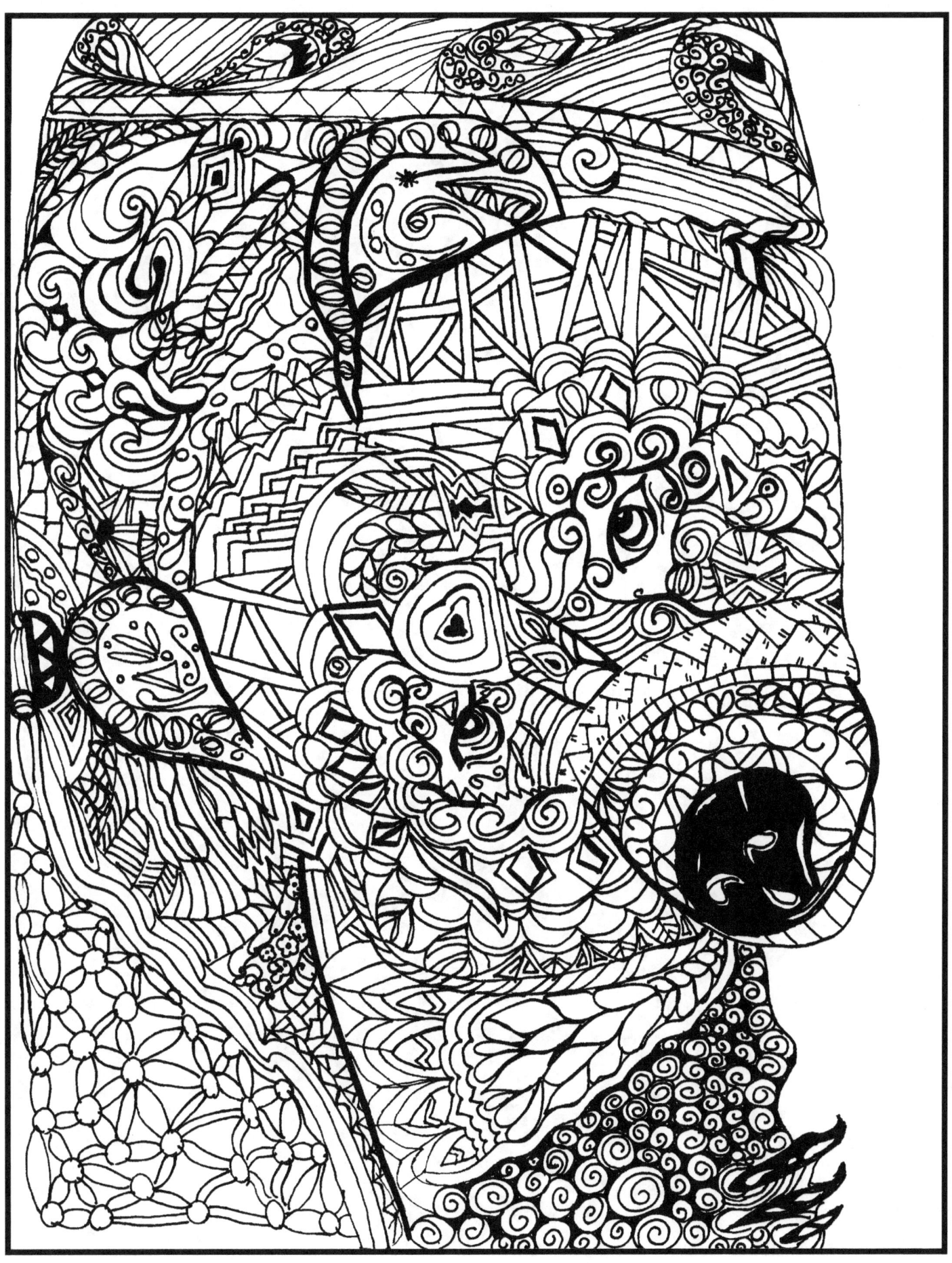

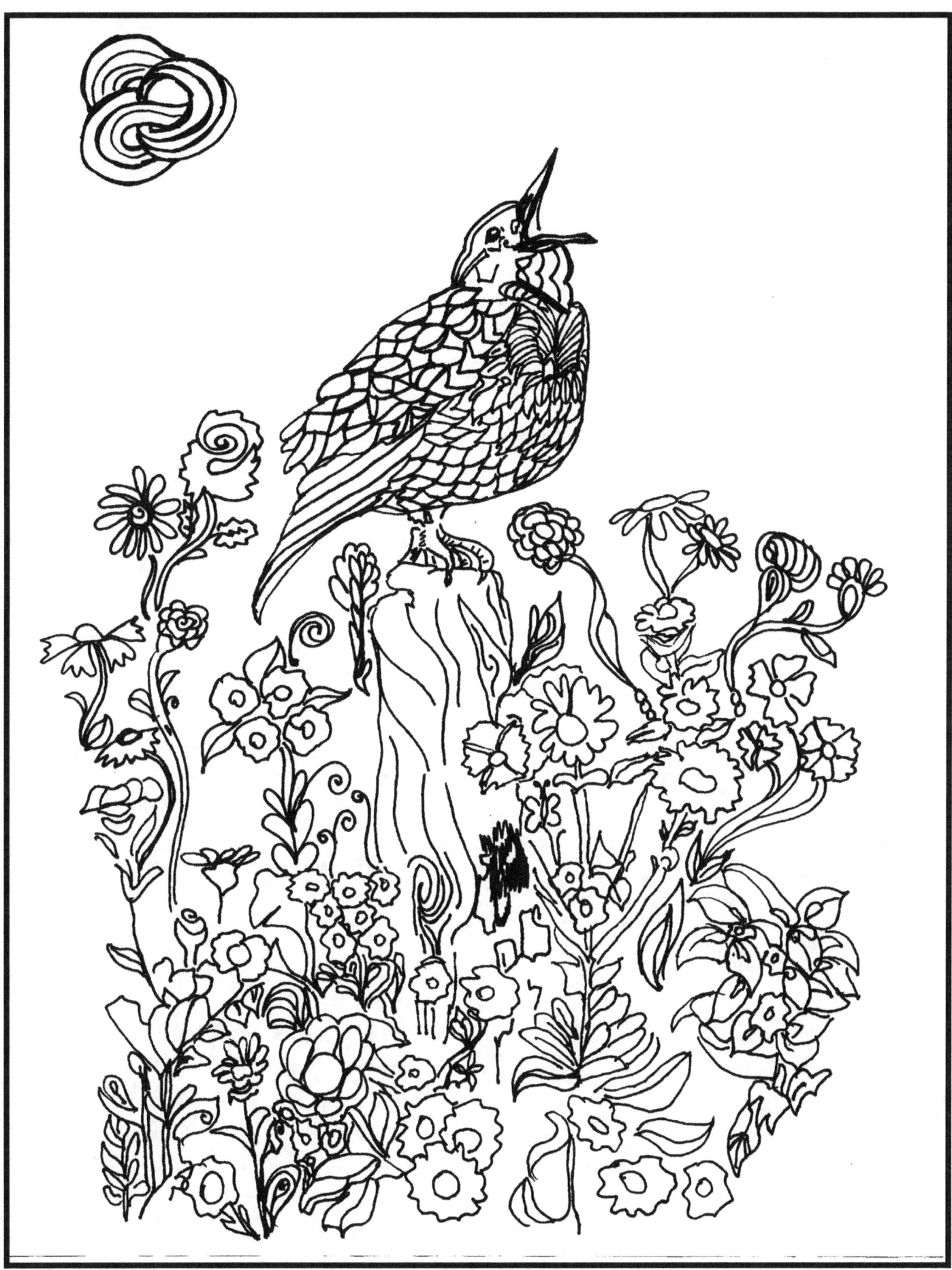

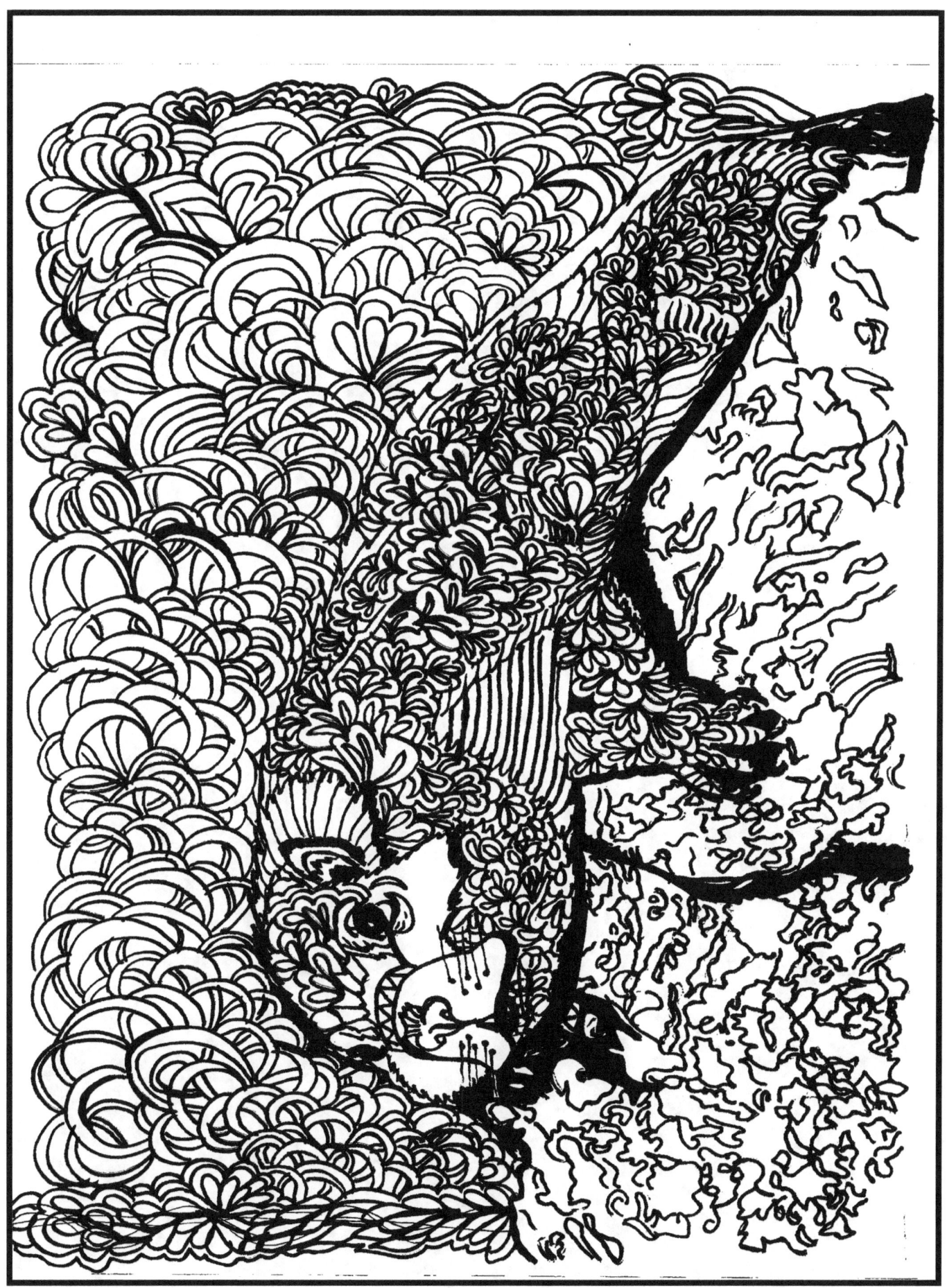

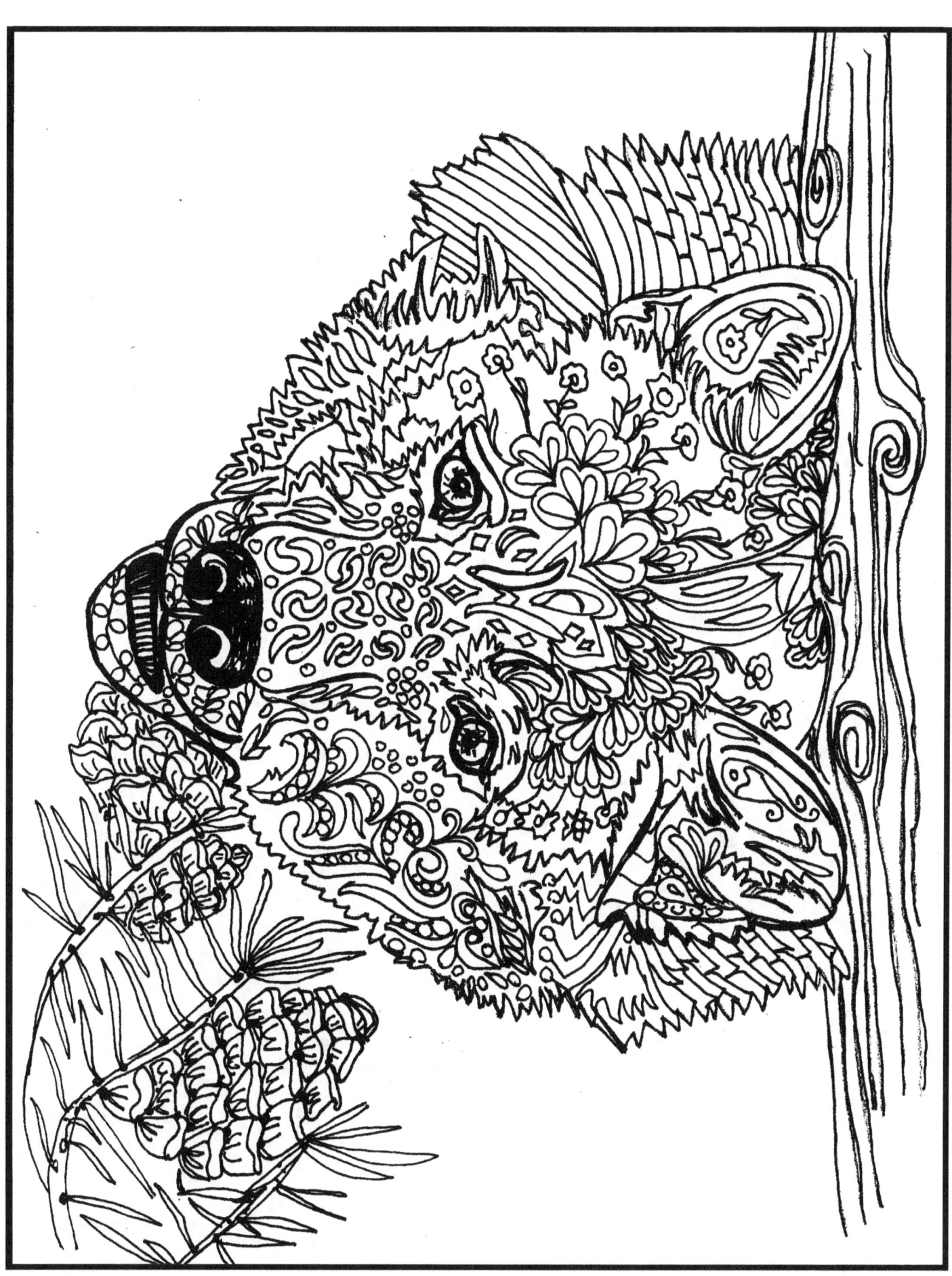

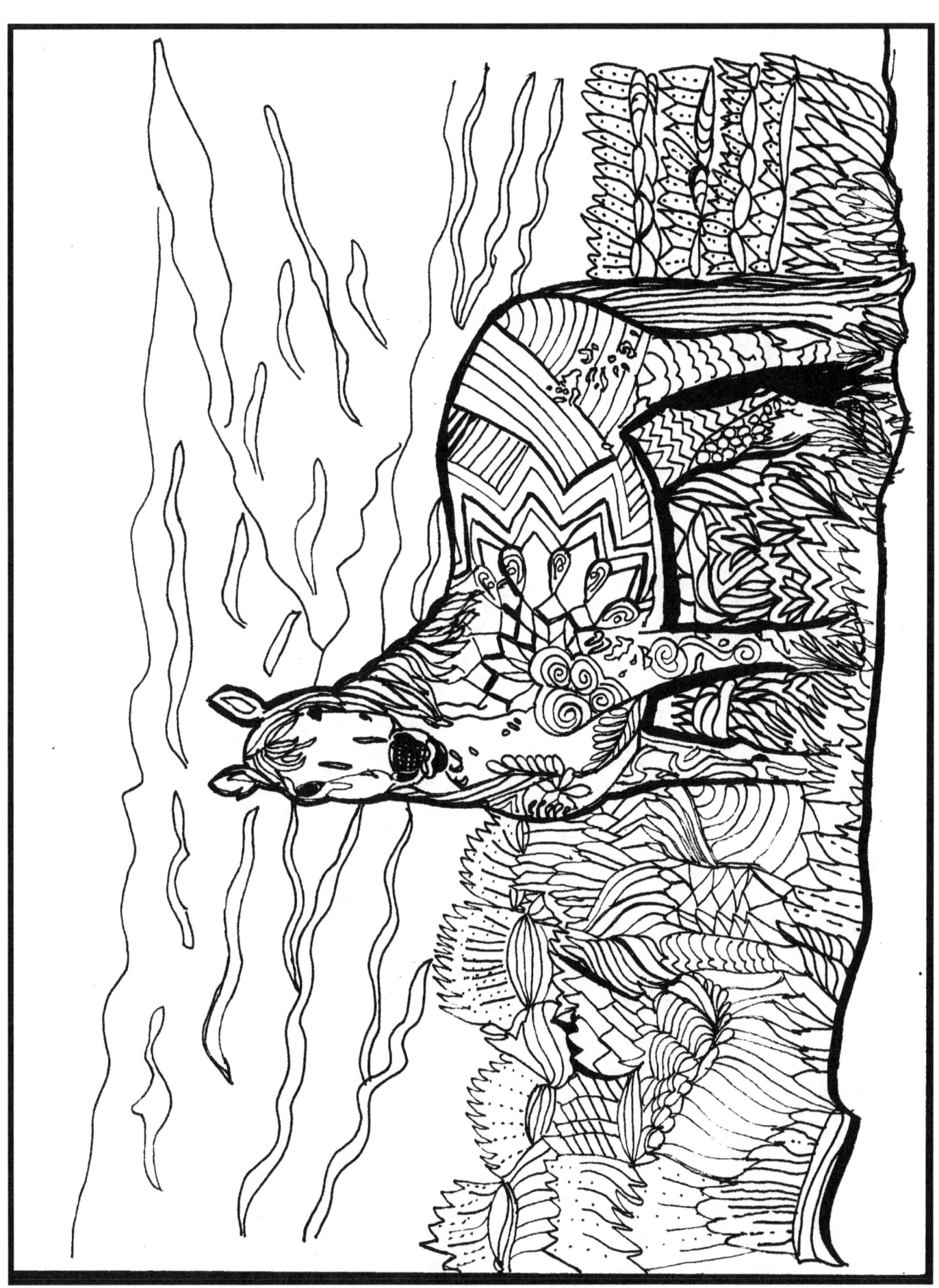

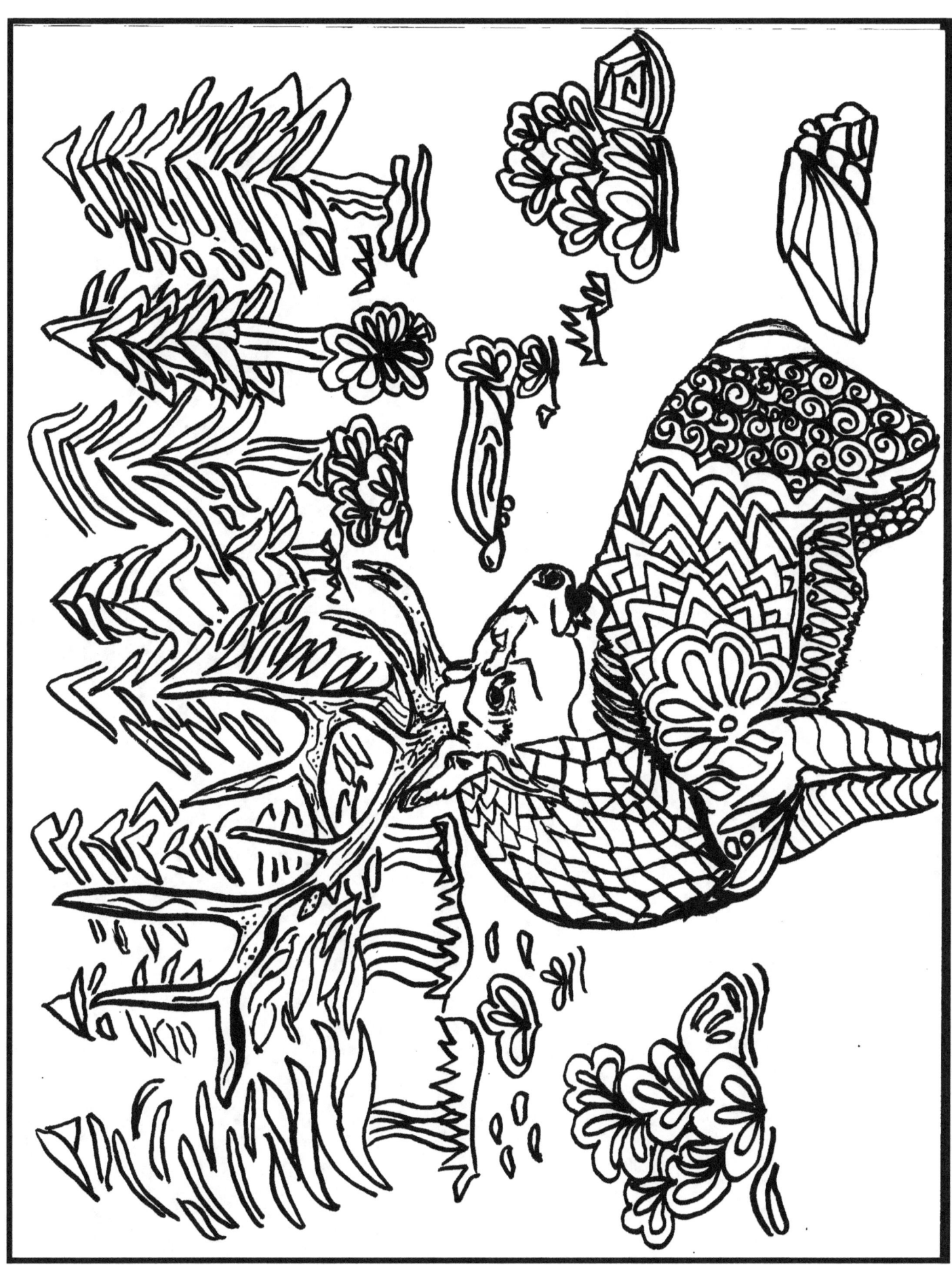

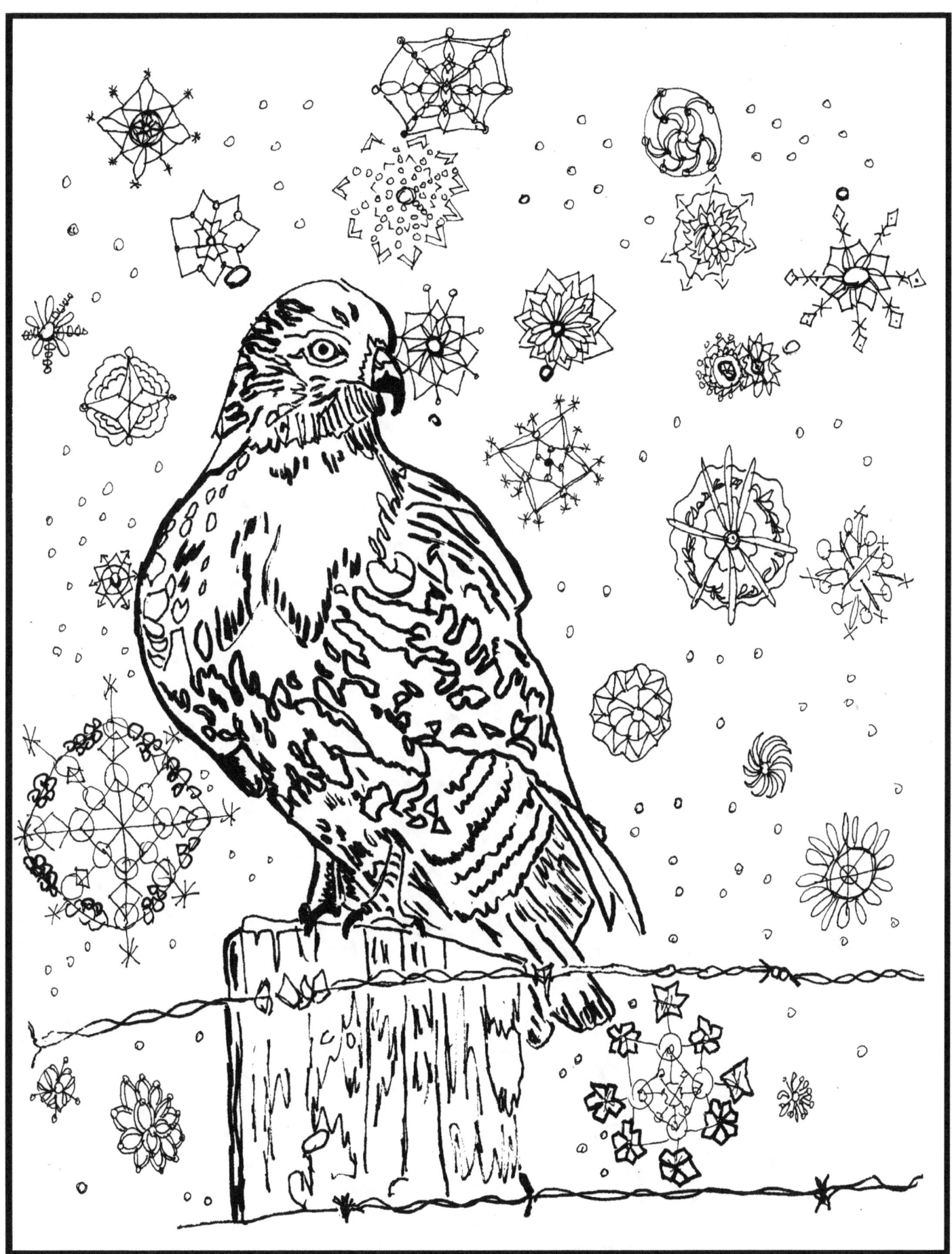

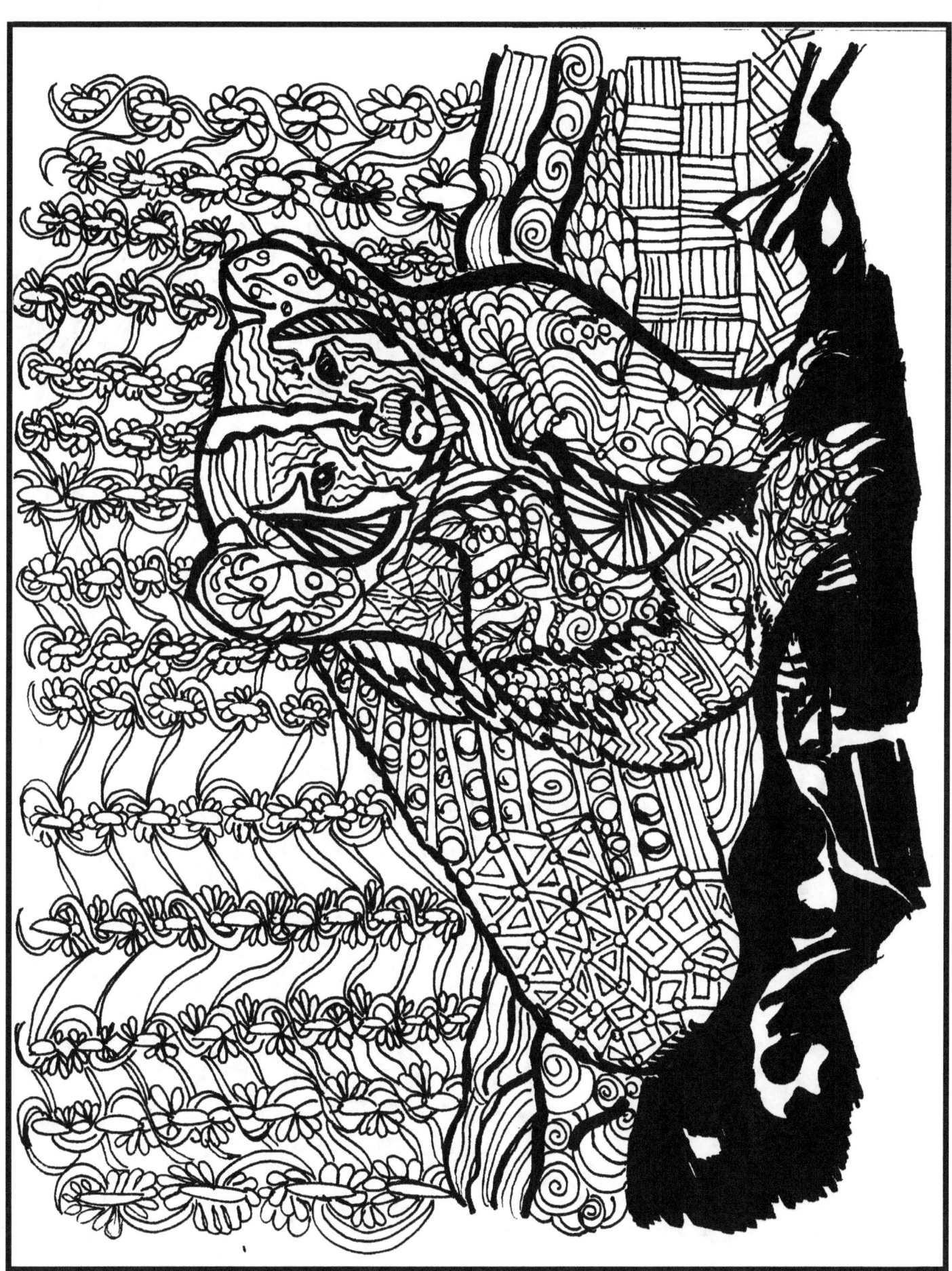

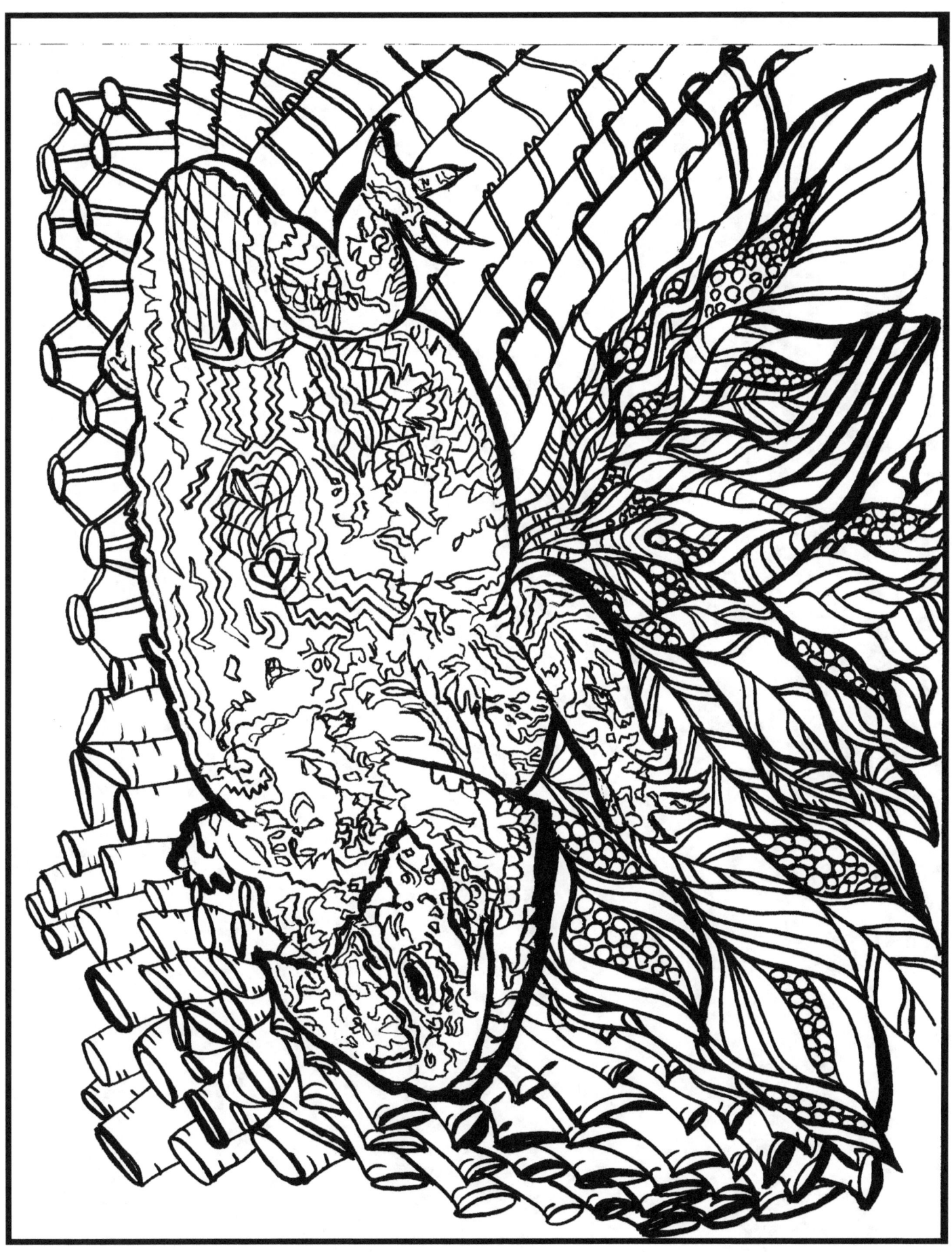

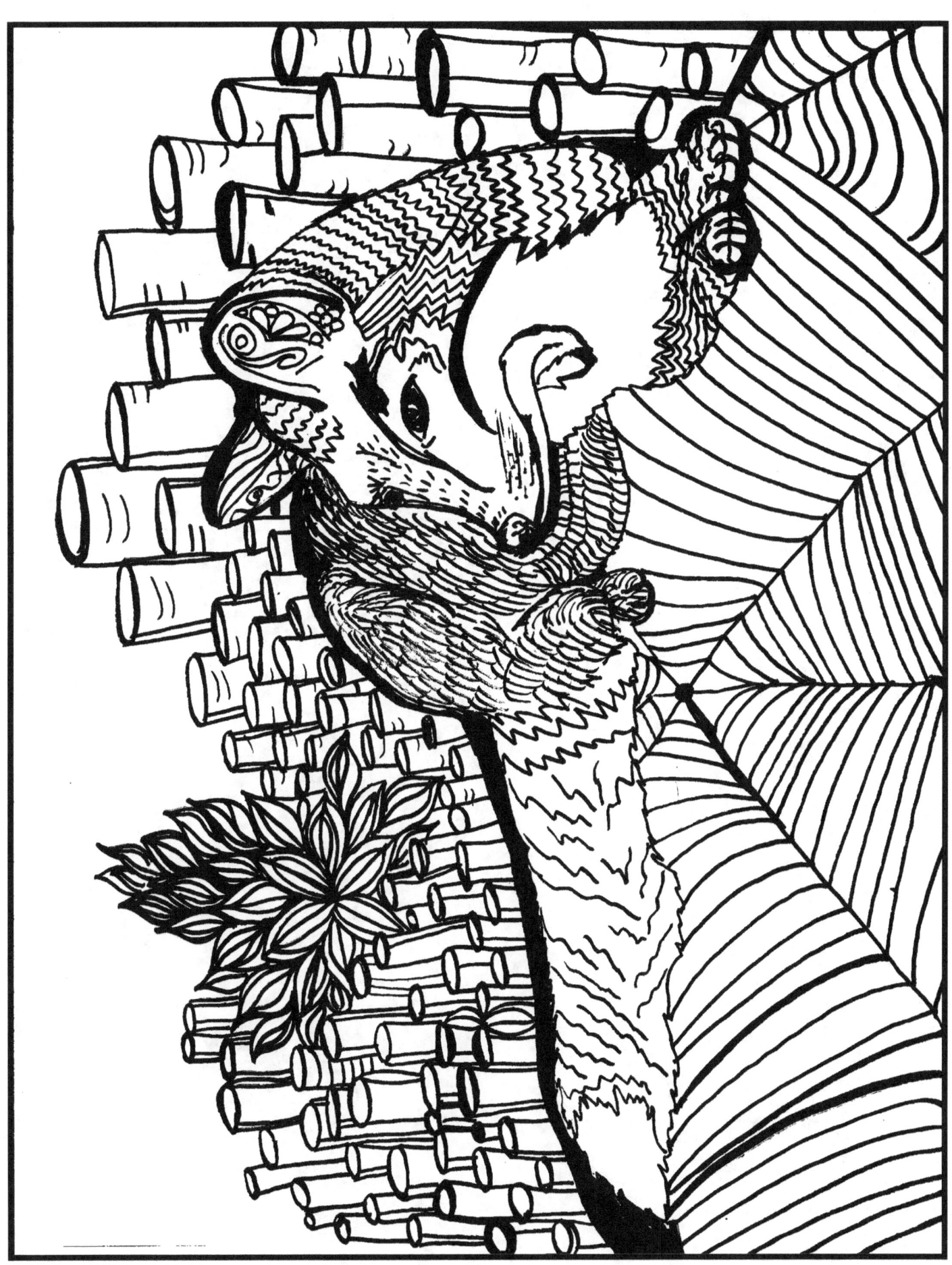

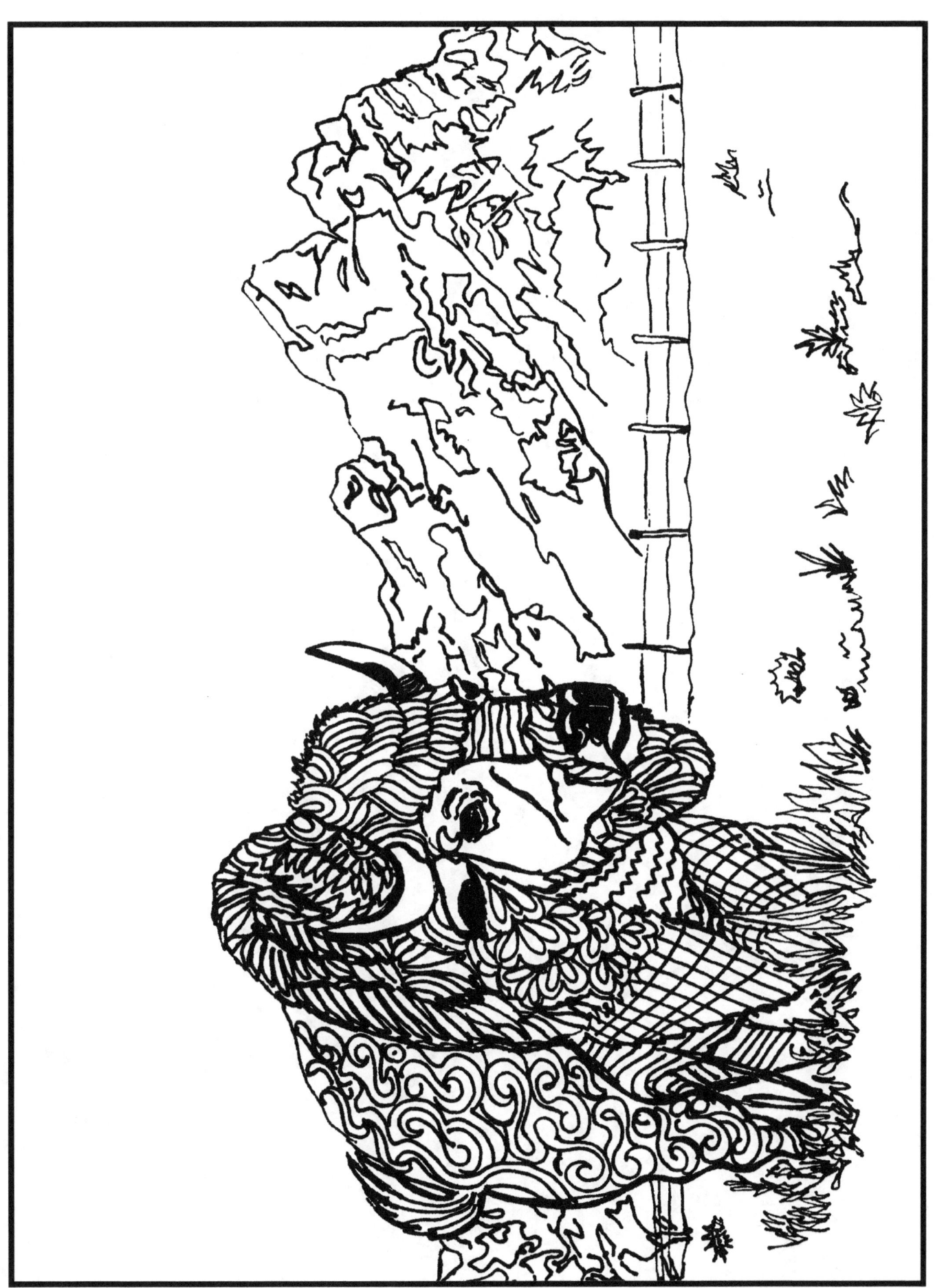

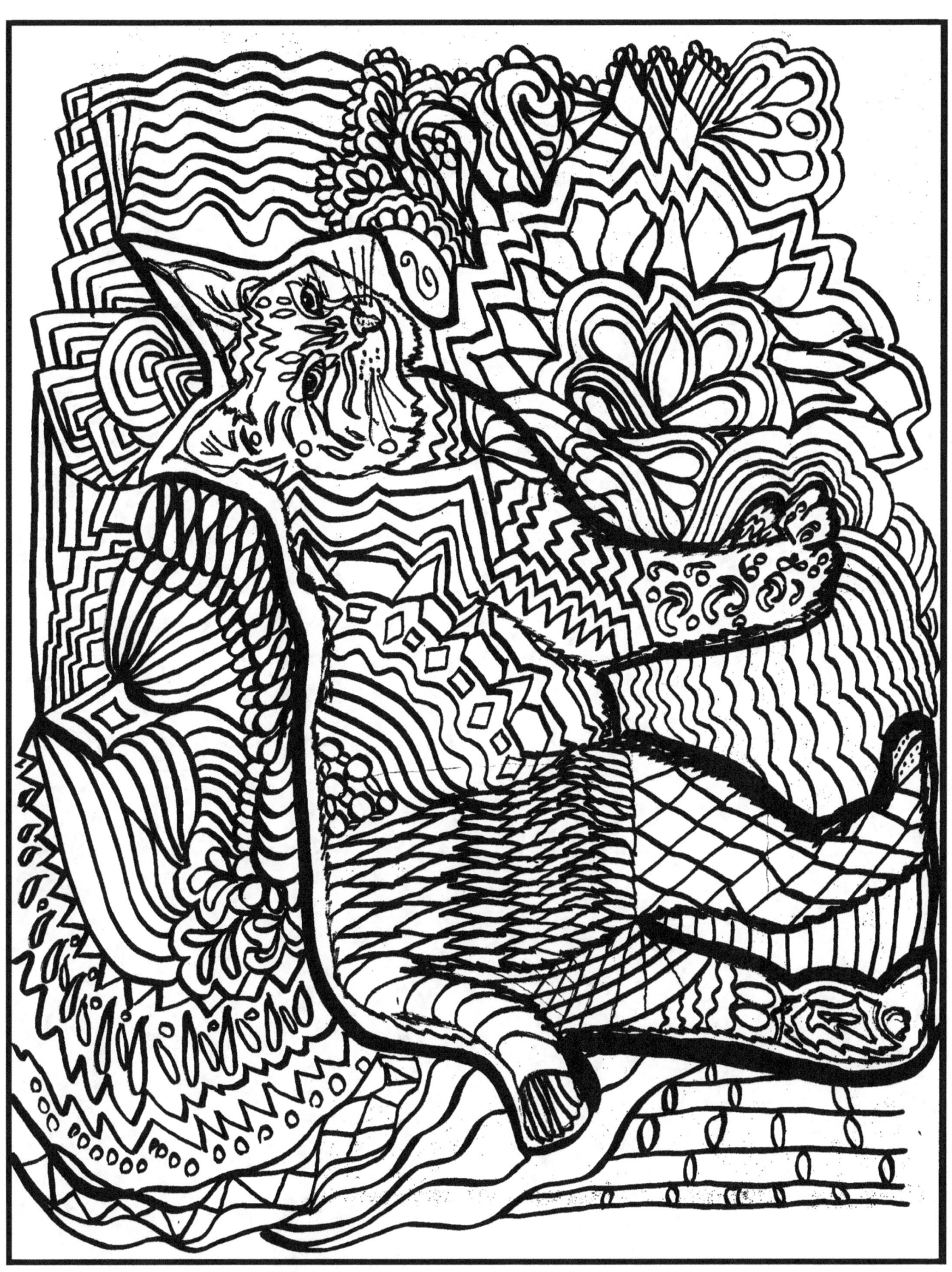

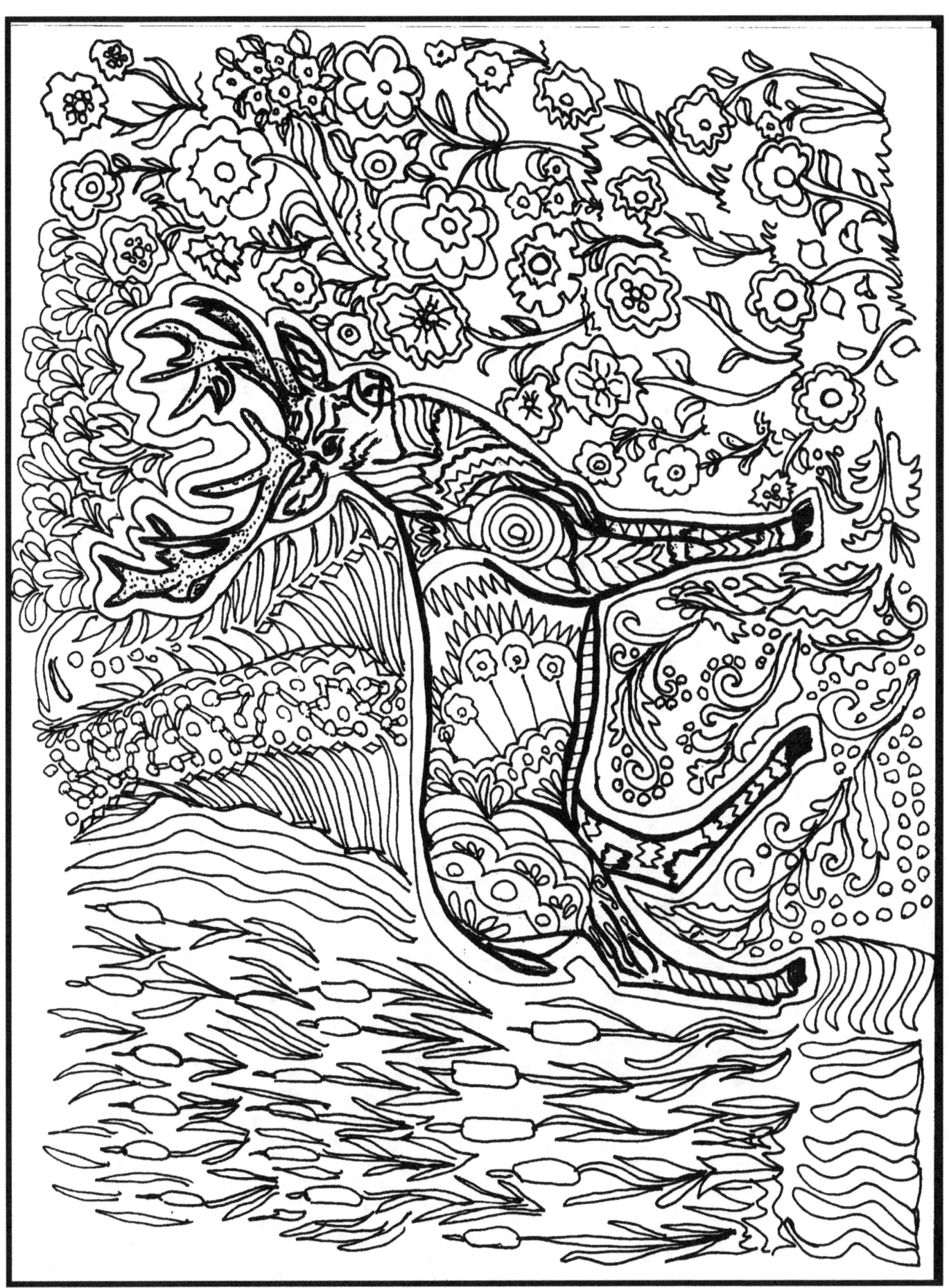

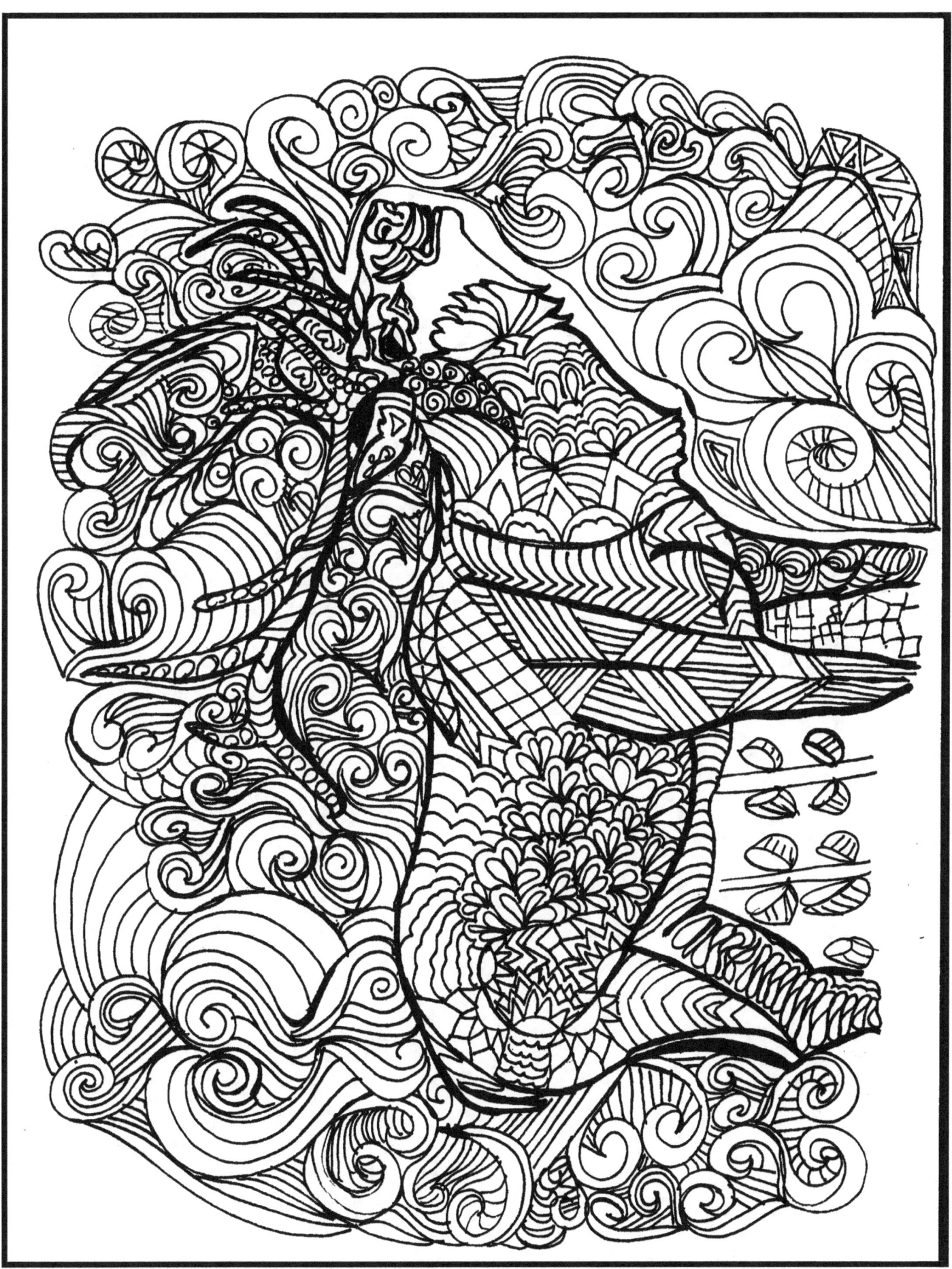

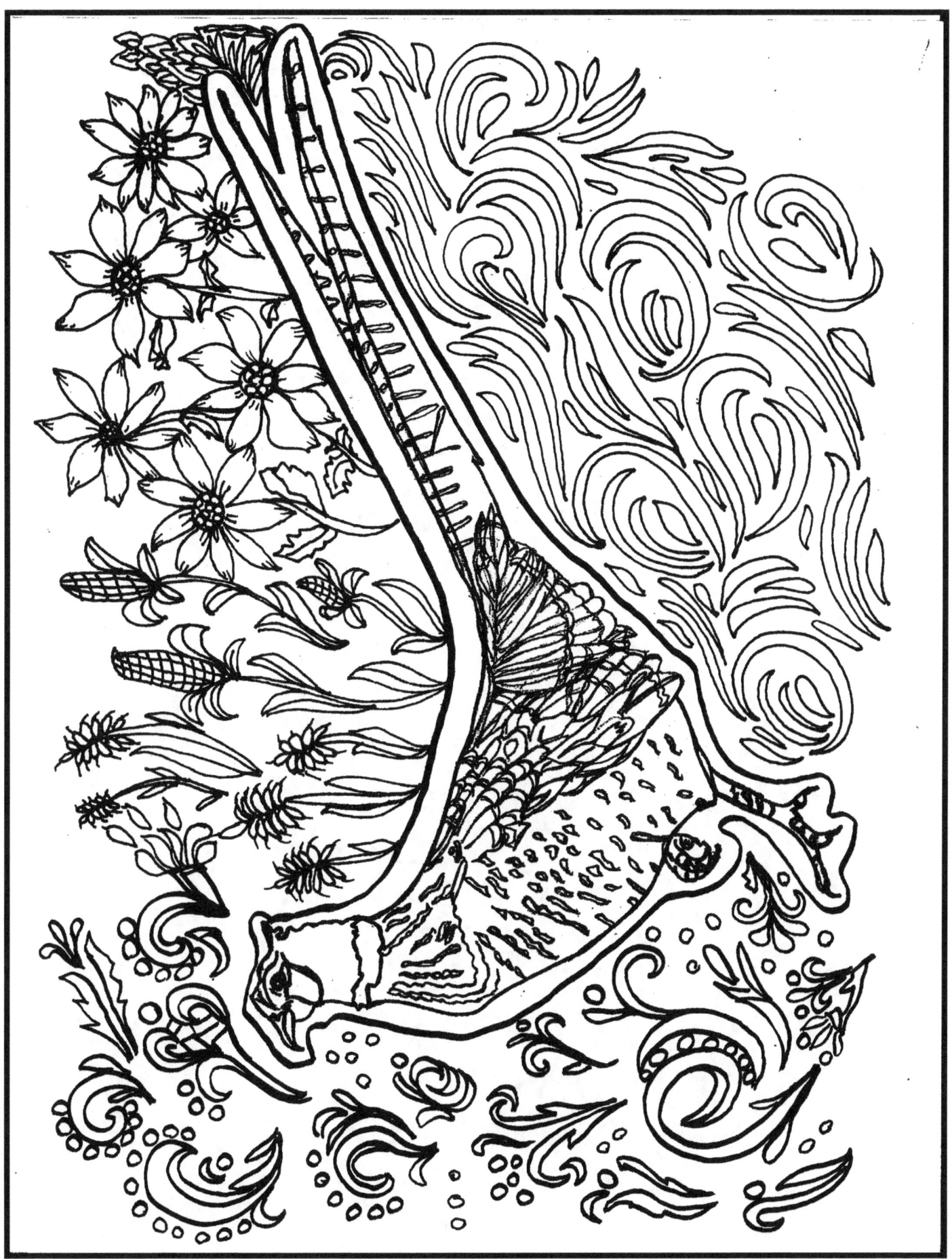

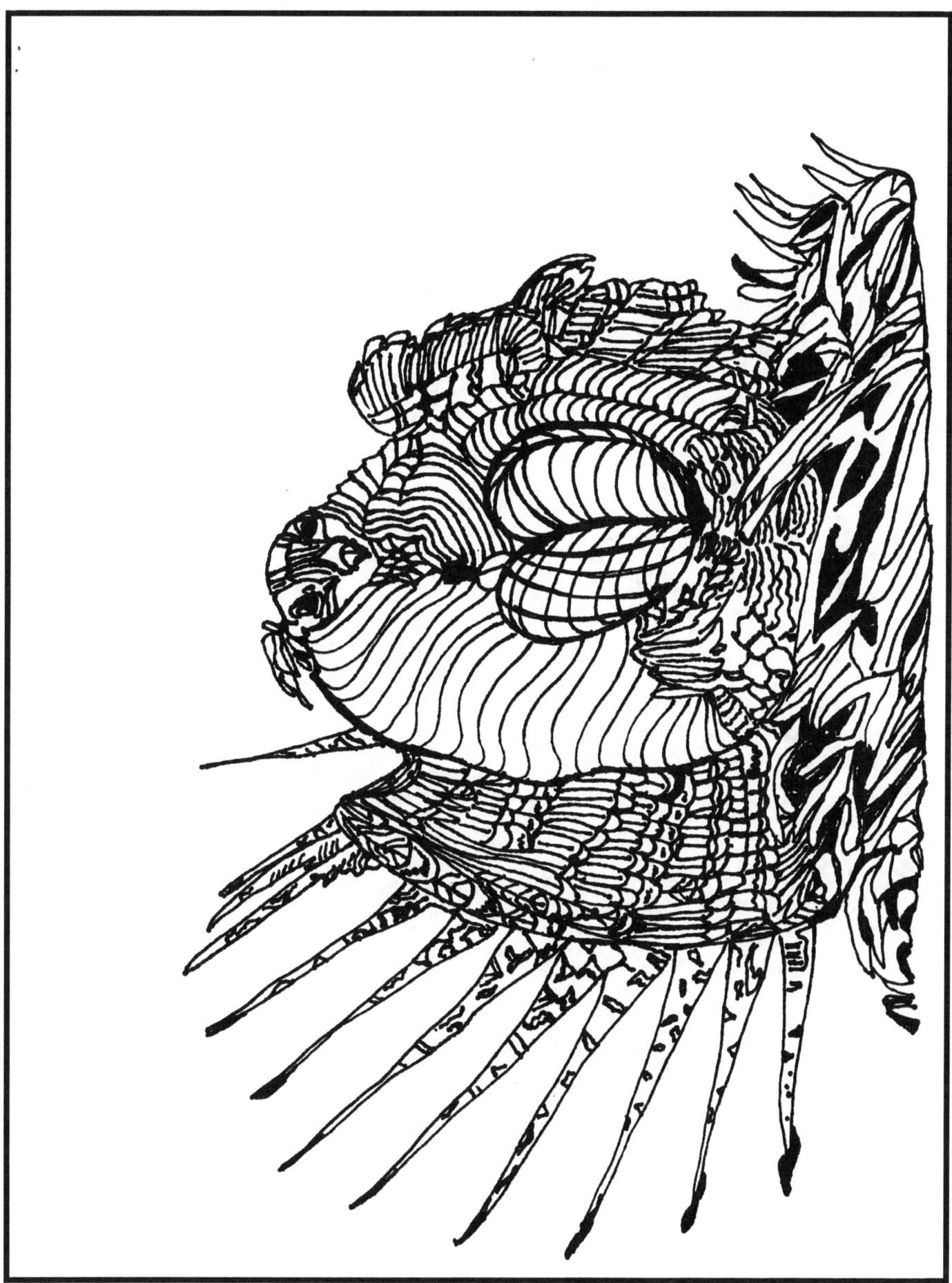

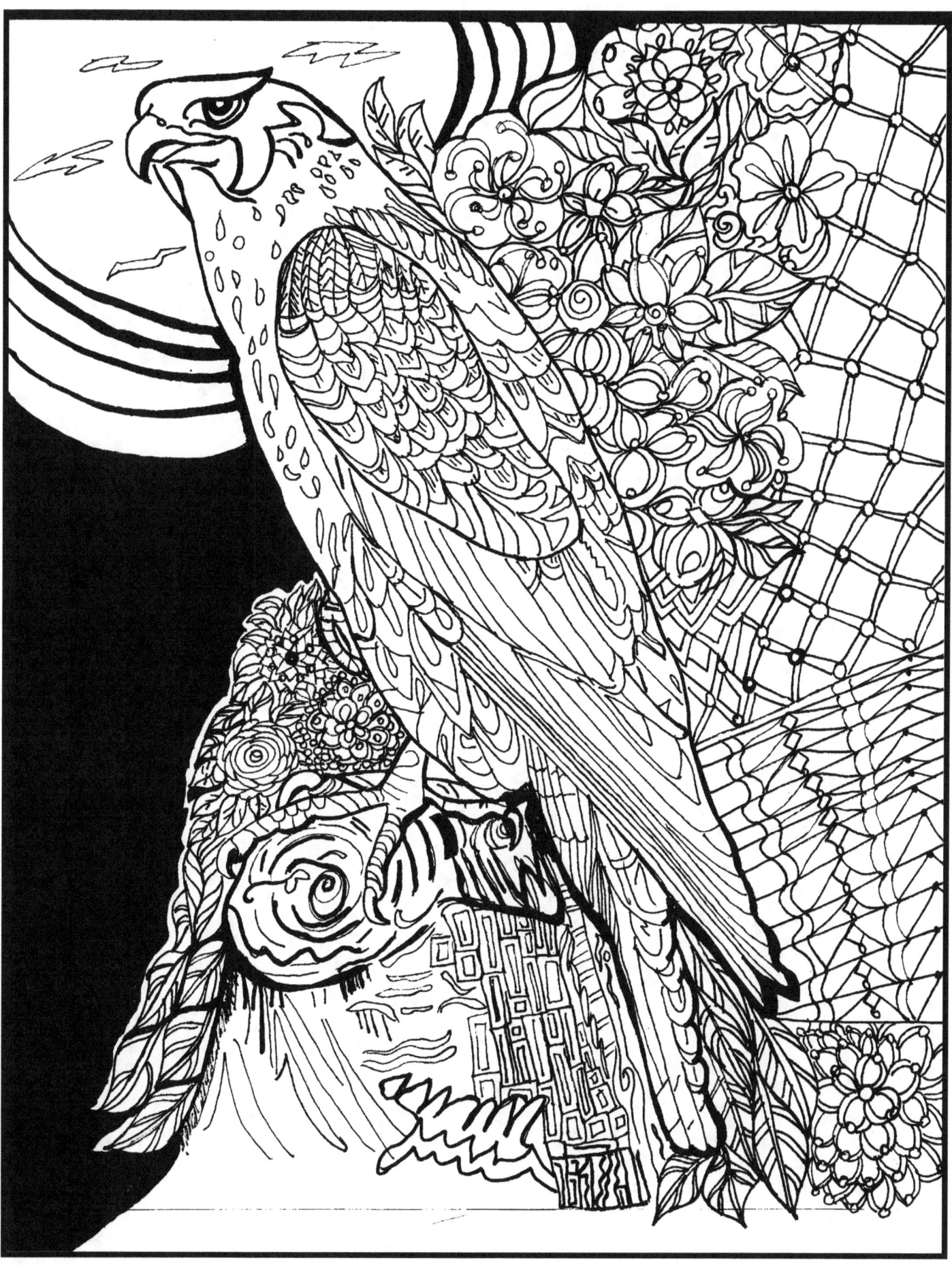

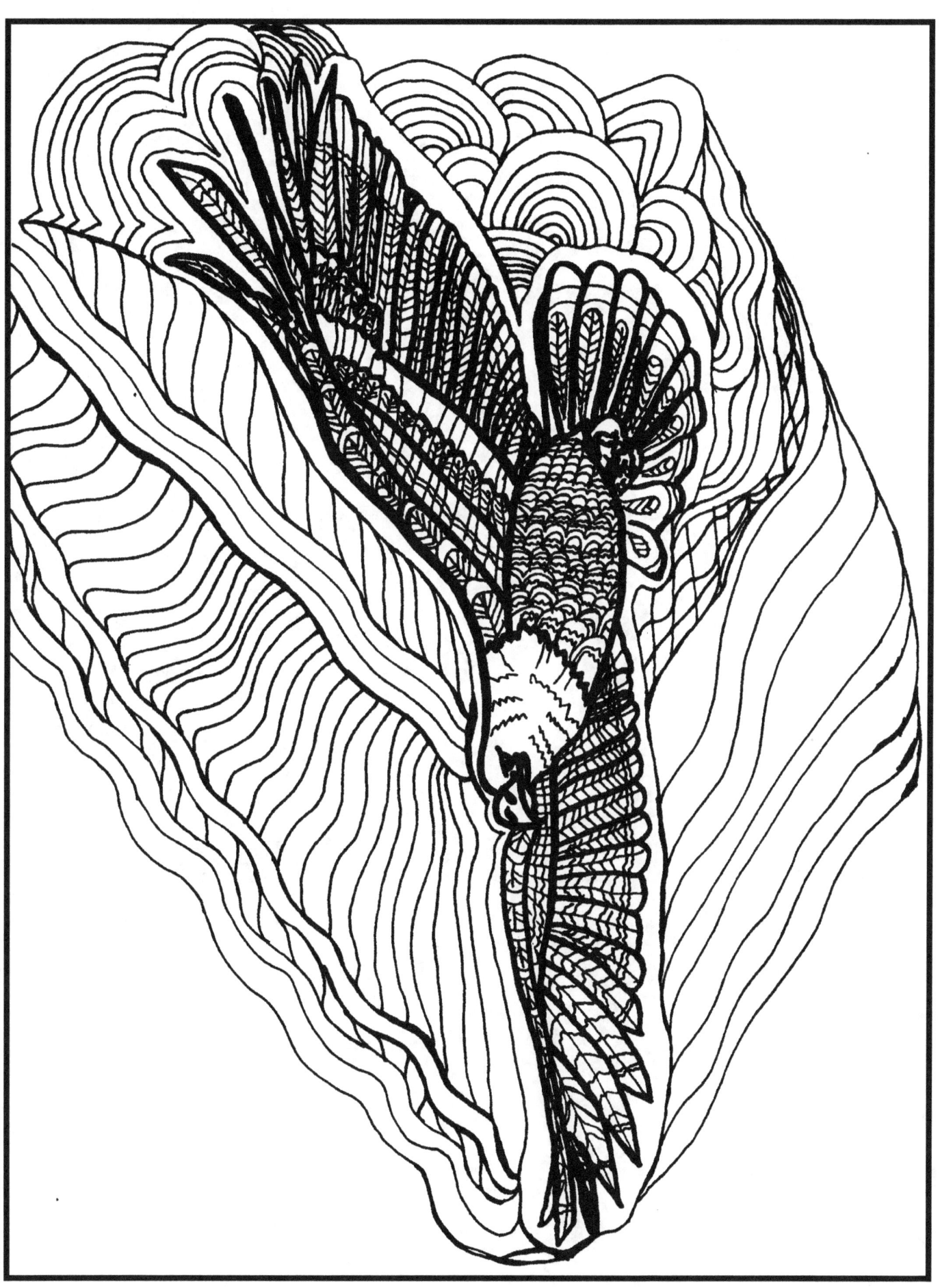

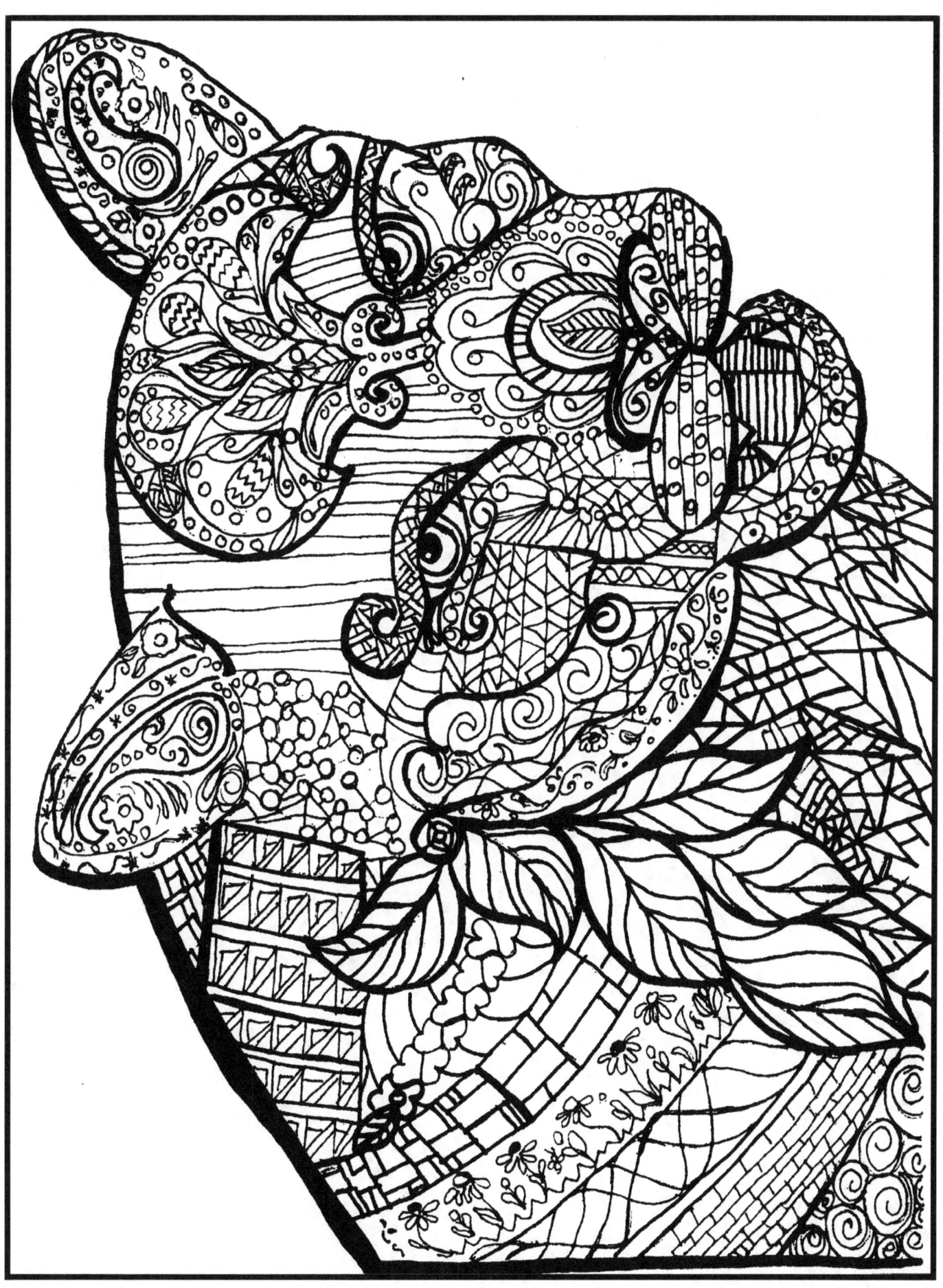

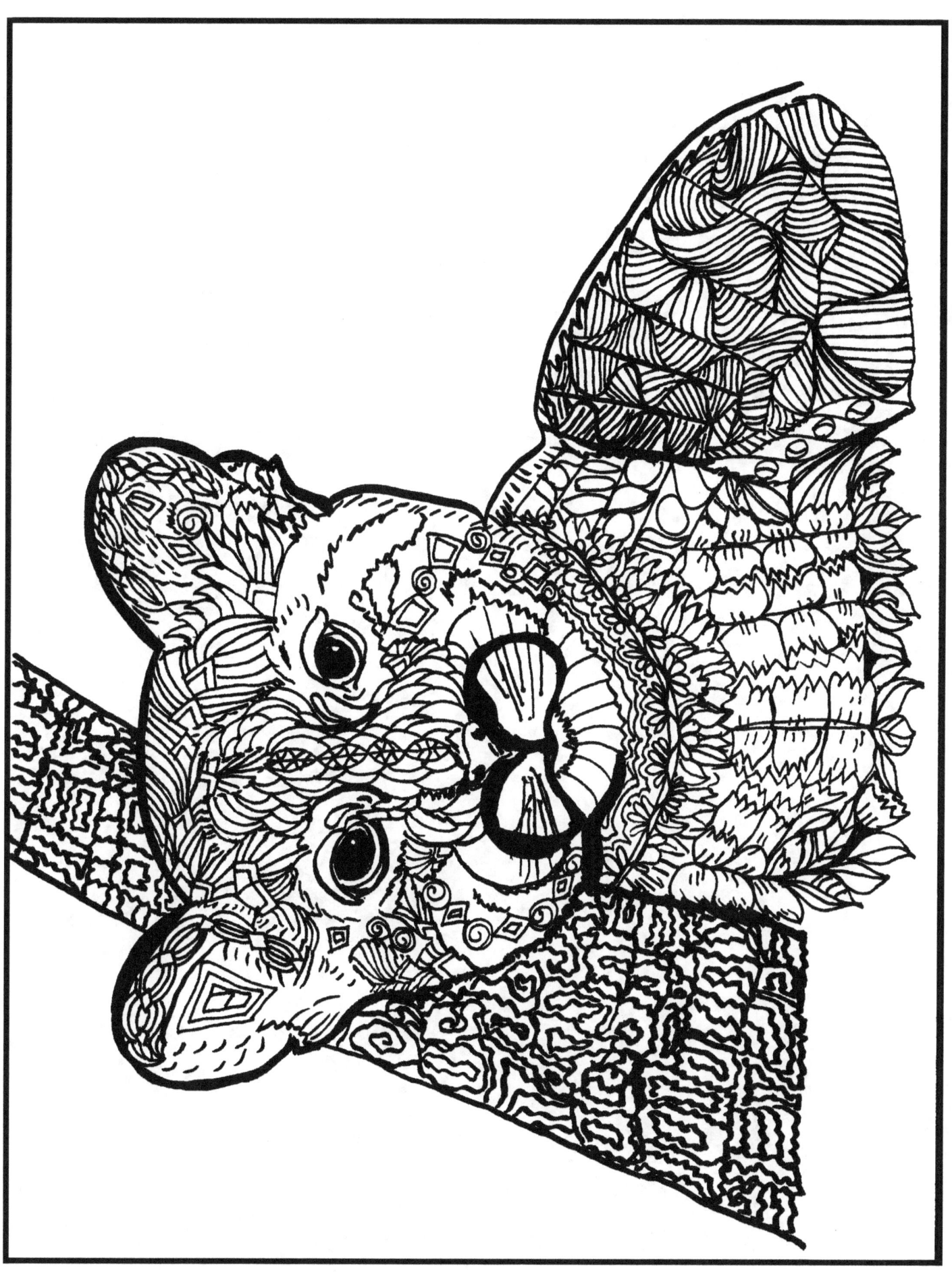

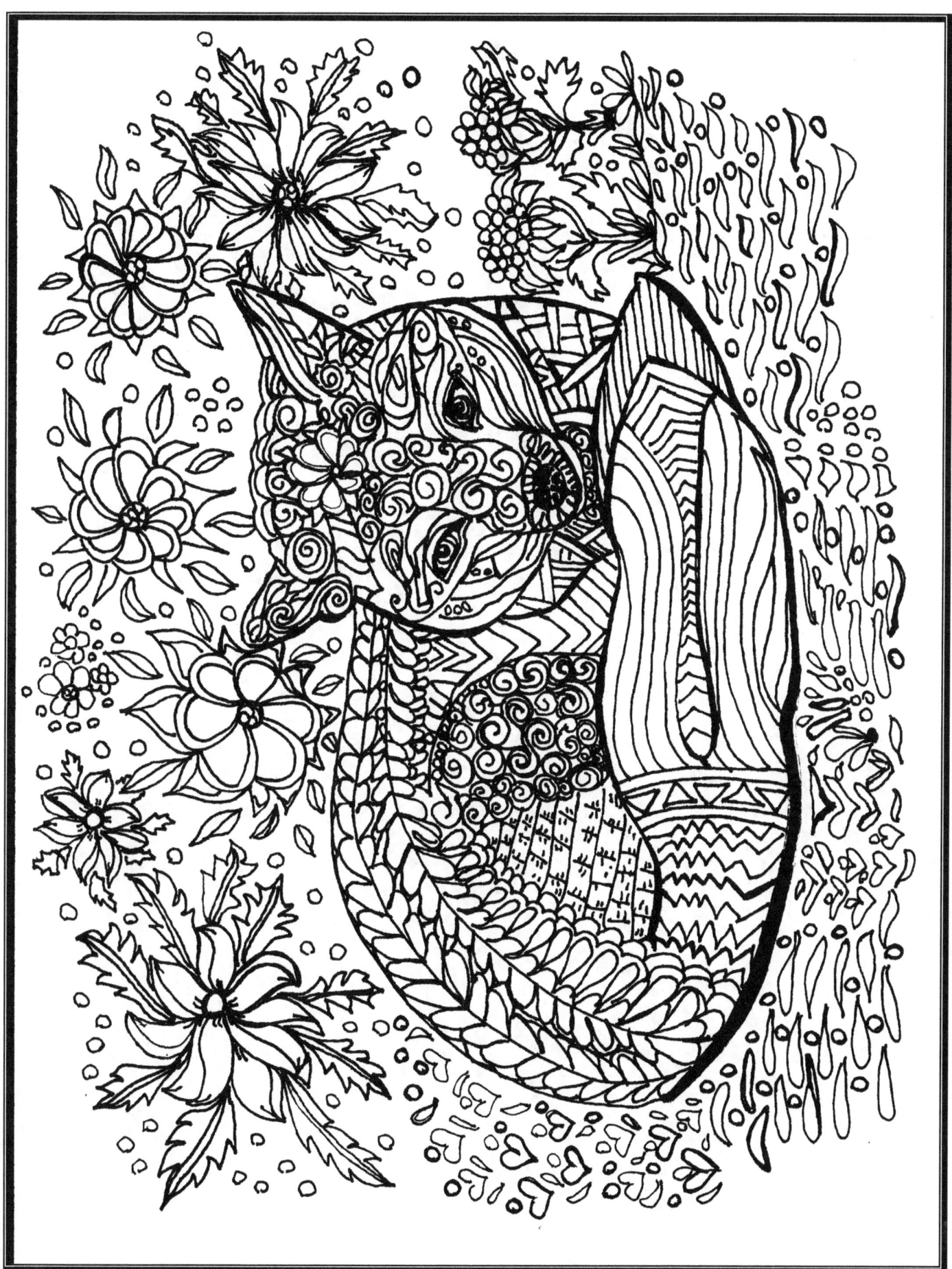

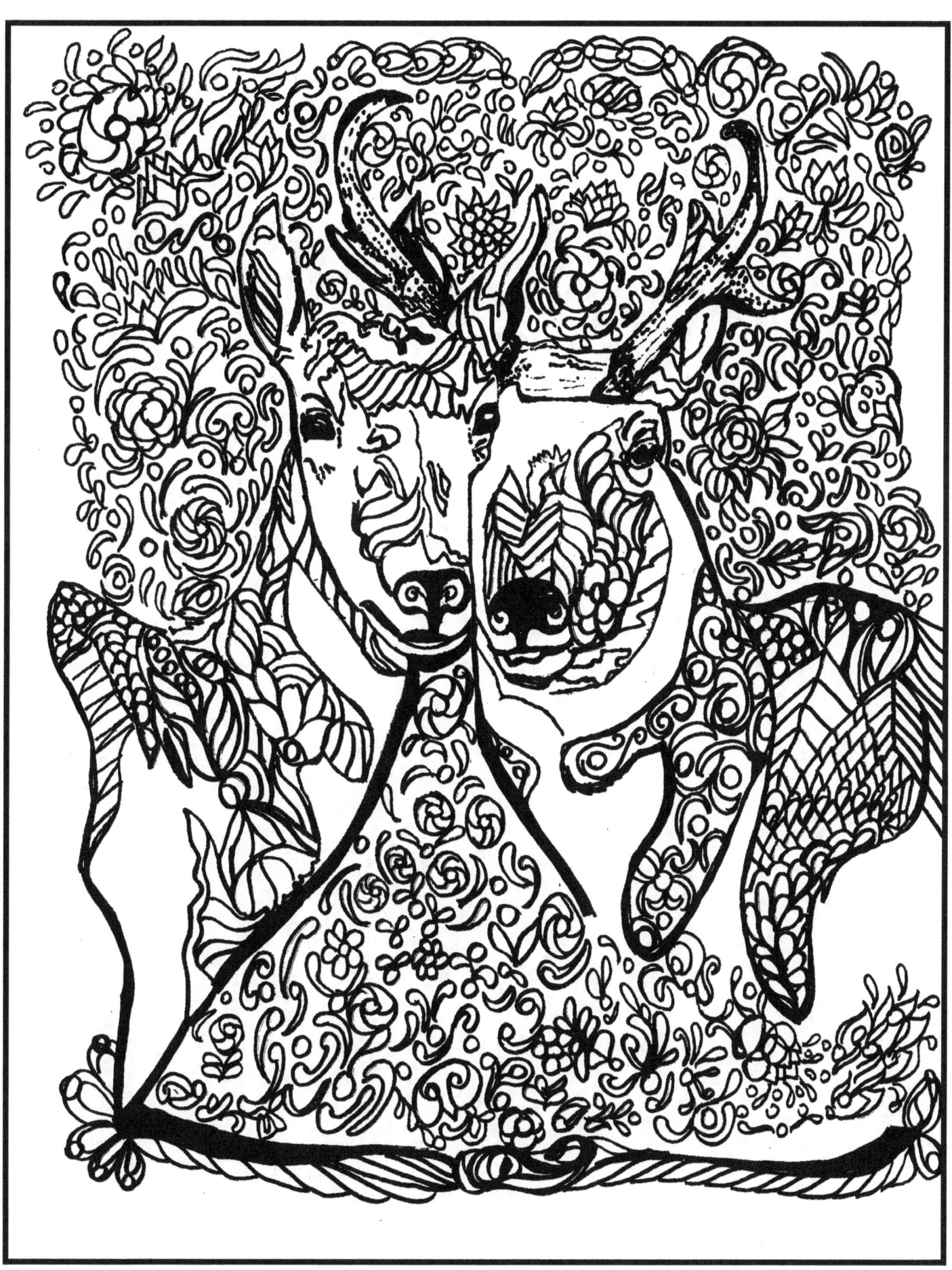

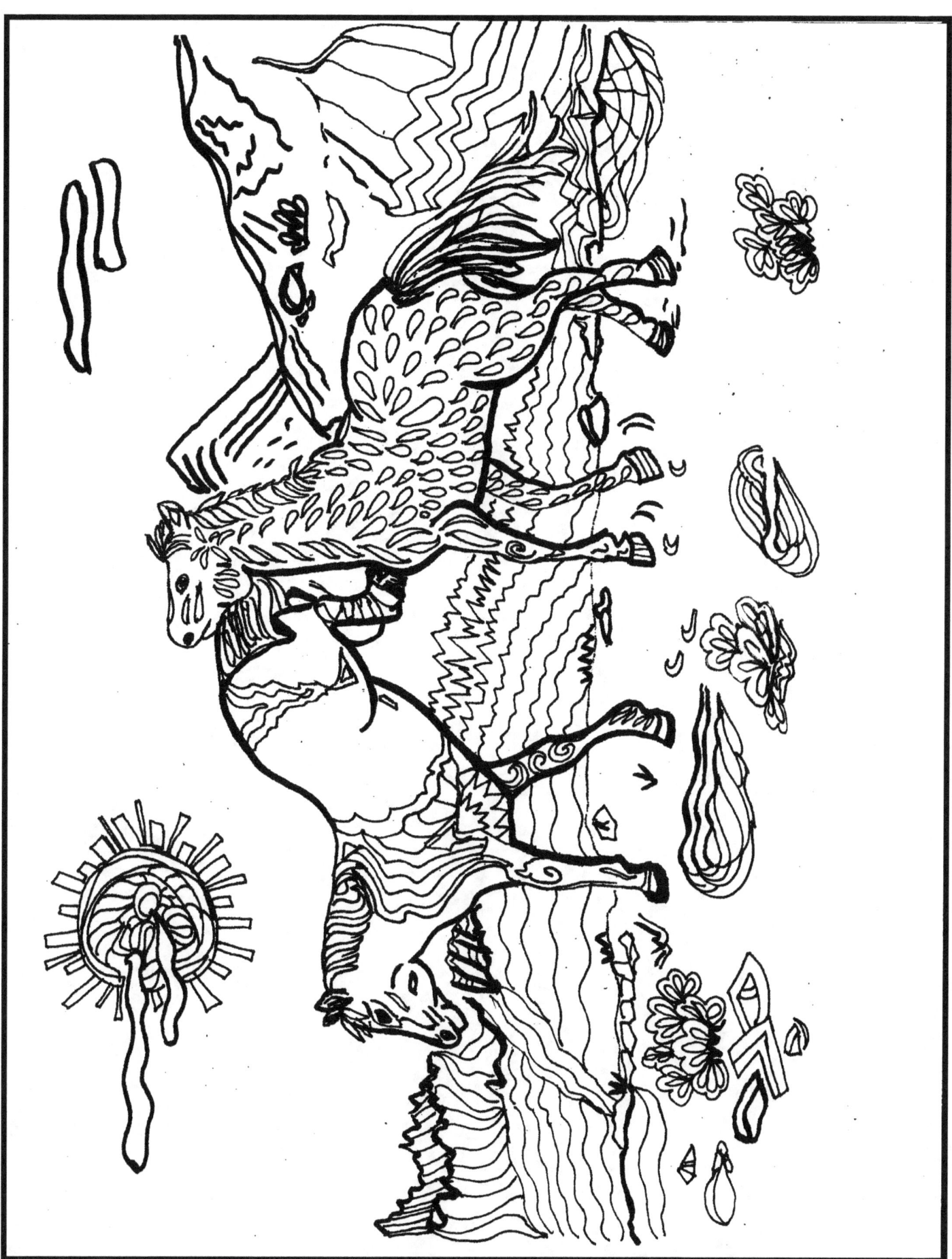

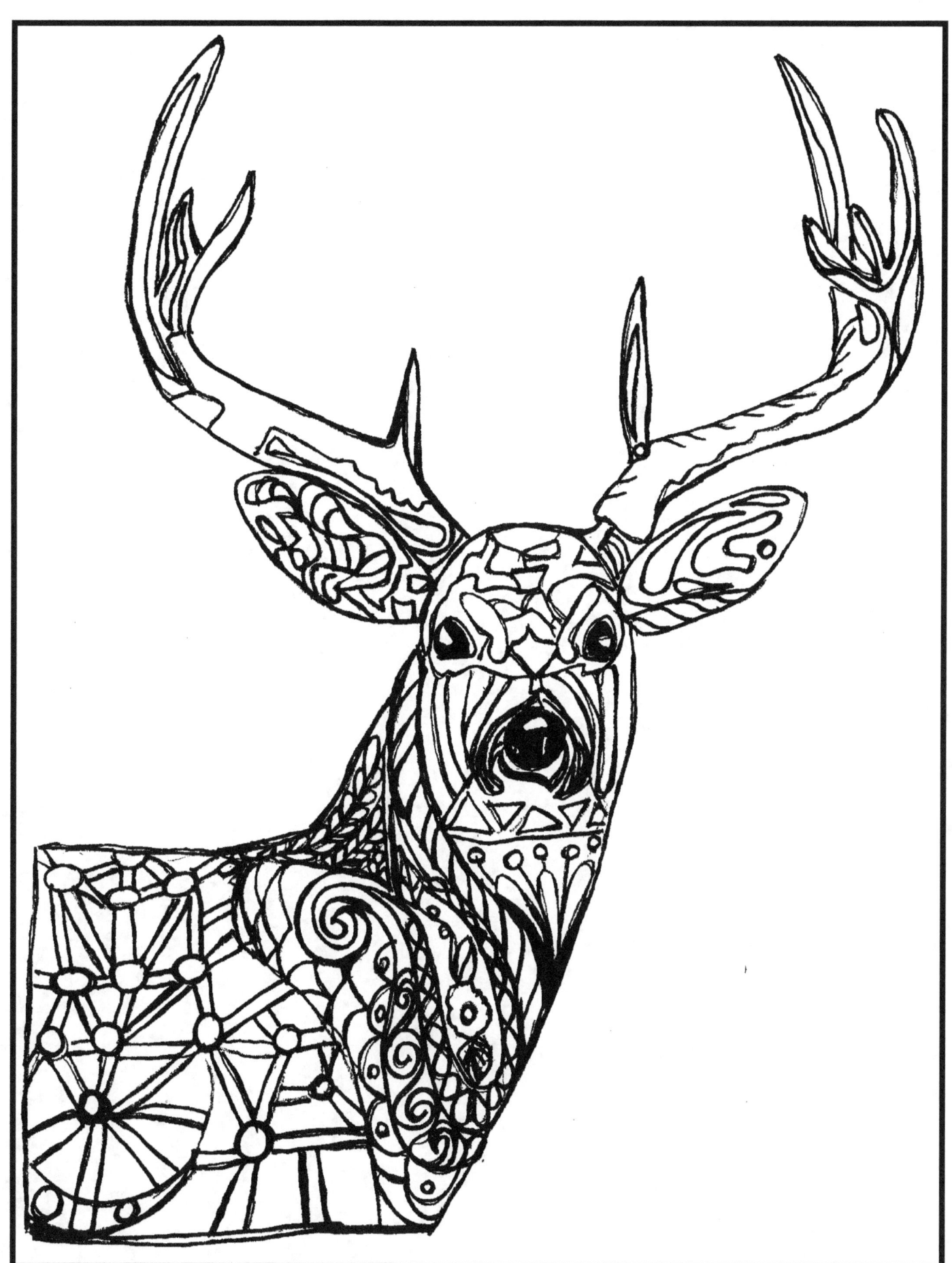

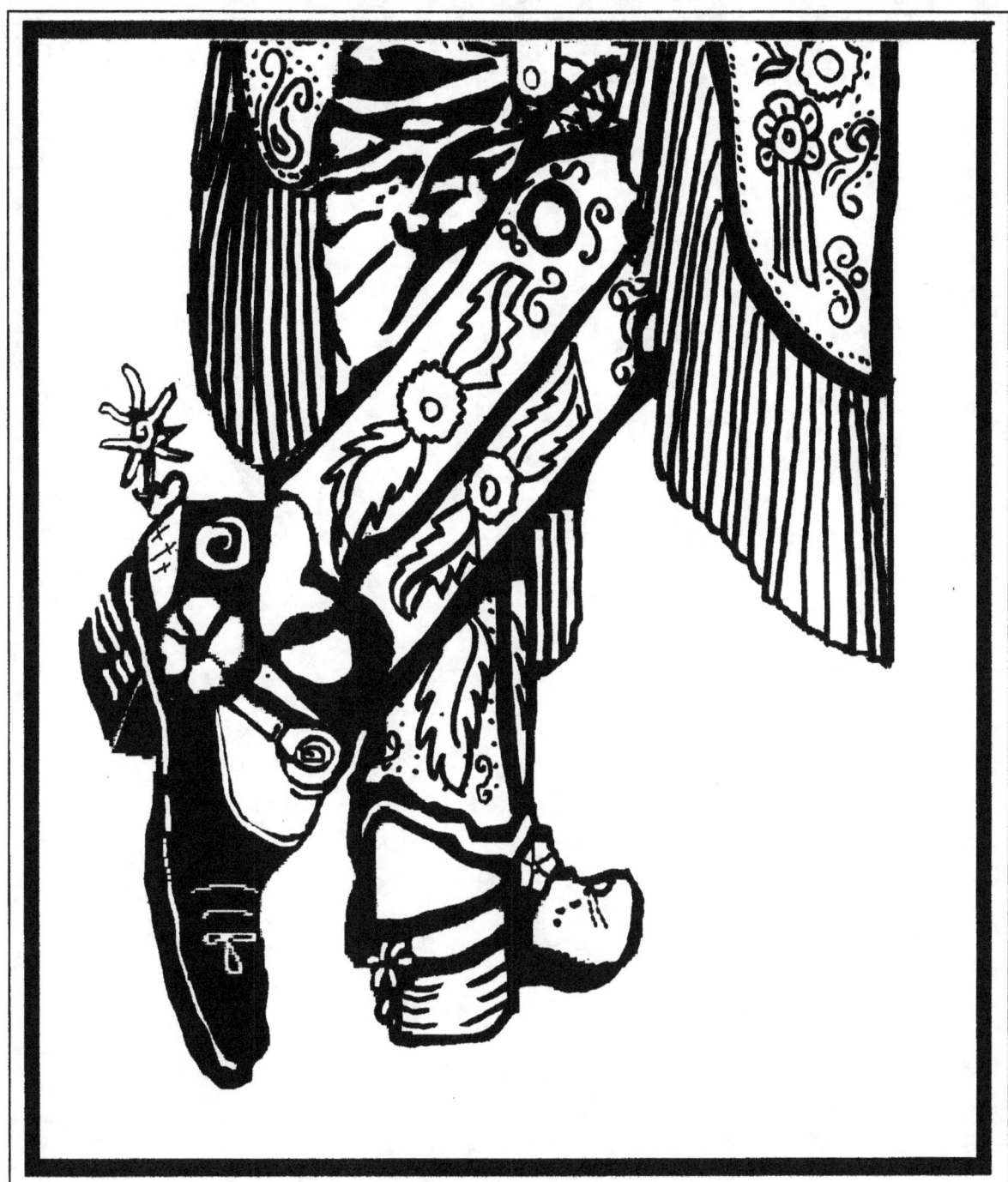

Coming Soon....

WYOMING
WILD
WEST

www.ingramcontent.com/pod-product-compliance
Lightning Source LLC
Chambersburg PA
CBHW080948170526
45158CB00008B/2416